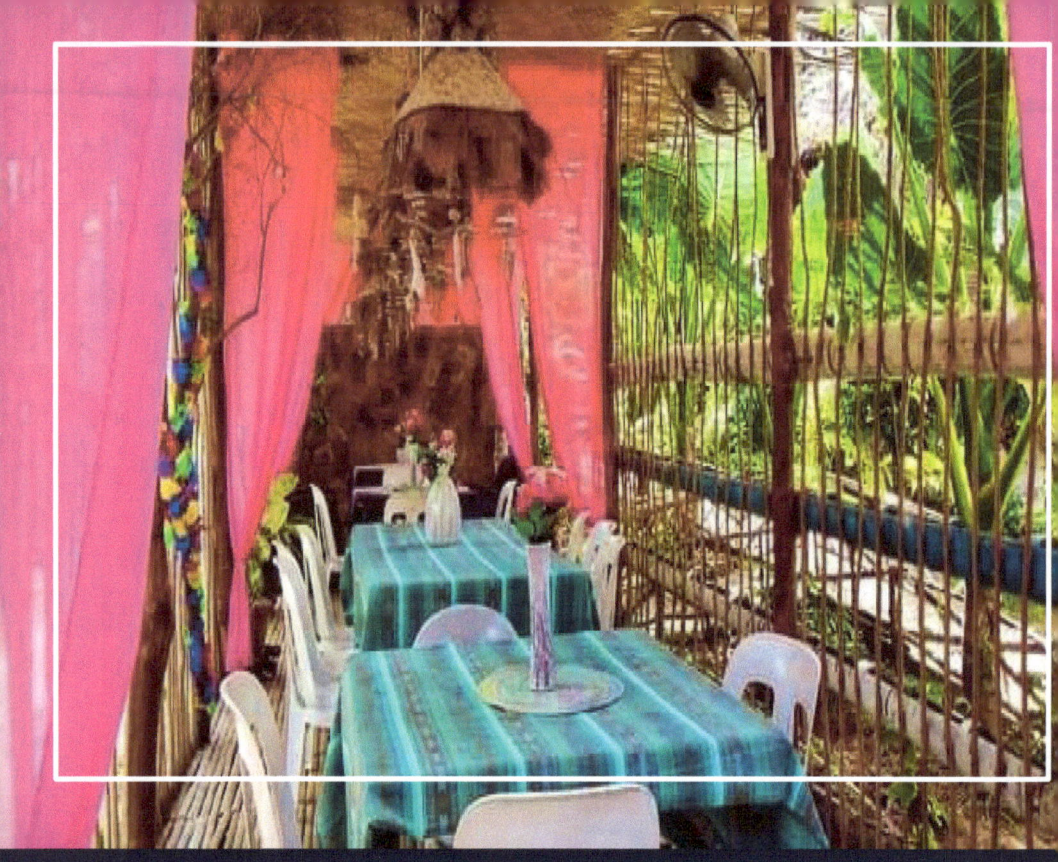

Set in the Native Homomoh Bar and Grill Restaurant Resort, the place offers fresh foods from the sea and a unique native elegant table arrangements and design.

Visiting and local tourist alike visit the place while en route to the famous church of Sulangan, other visitors just drop by the place for a refreshing view of the beach and the great ambiance offered by the place.

The Homomoh Bar and Grill Restaurant Resort is located near a beautiful beach just a few walk to the back side of the resort.

Simplicity and Elegance with nature brings peace of mind.

Photo Image by Mae Abueme at Sulangan, Guiuan Eastern Samar

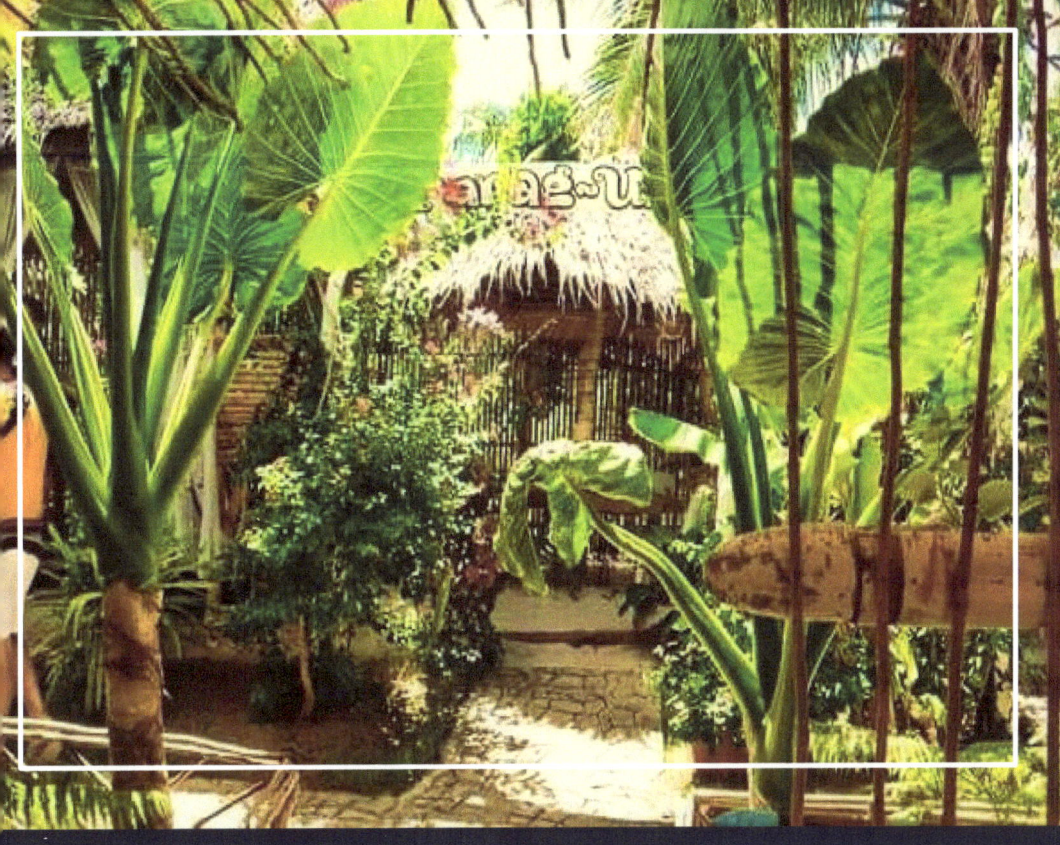

A combination of natural and native materials creates for this wonderful Nipa Huts where food is served along with native plants surrounding the place.

The Nipa Huts are named individually from the local dialects and in reference to local fisher folk's terms about local lifestyles and native culture.

Visitors can chose from a variety of local sea foods, grilled meat and chicken including a variety of fruit juice for serving.

The place is great for family recreation amid the busy life in the urban world.

Photo Image by Mae Abueme at Sulangan, Guiuan Eastern Samar

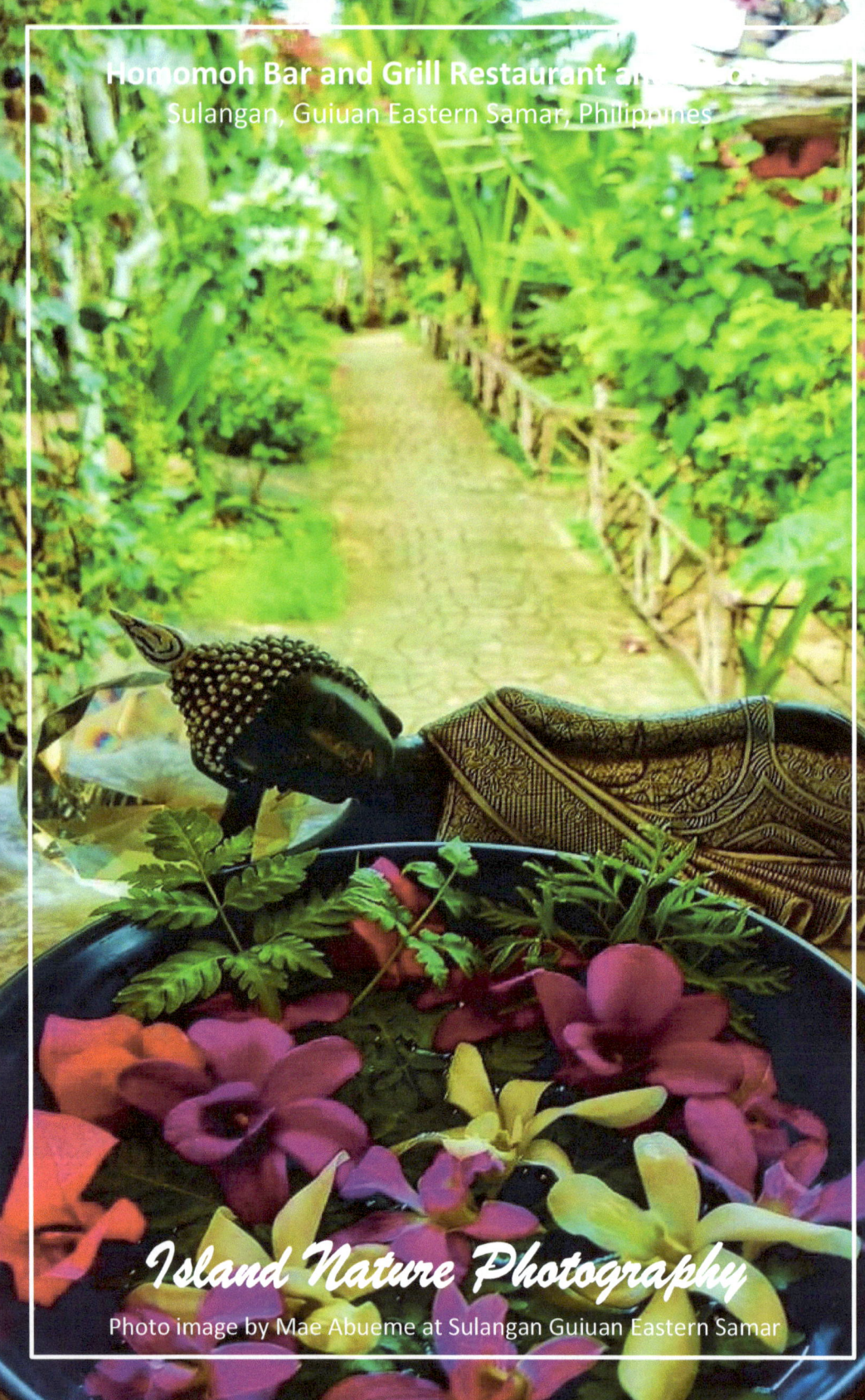

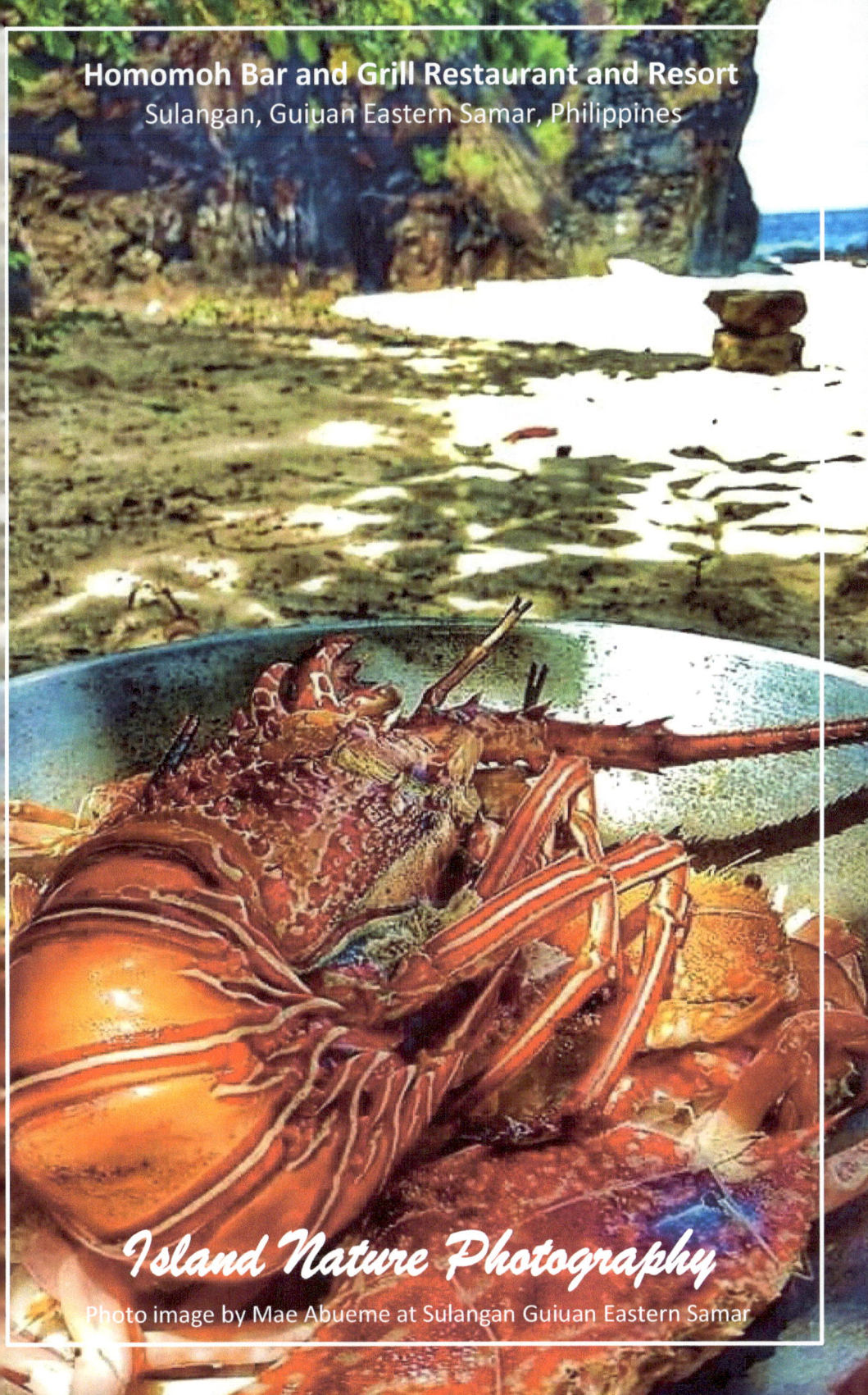

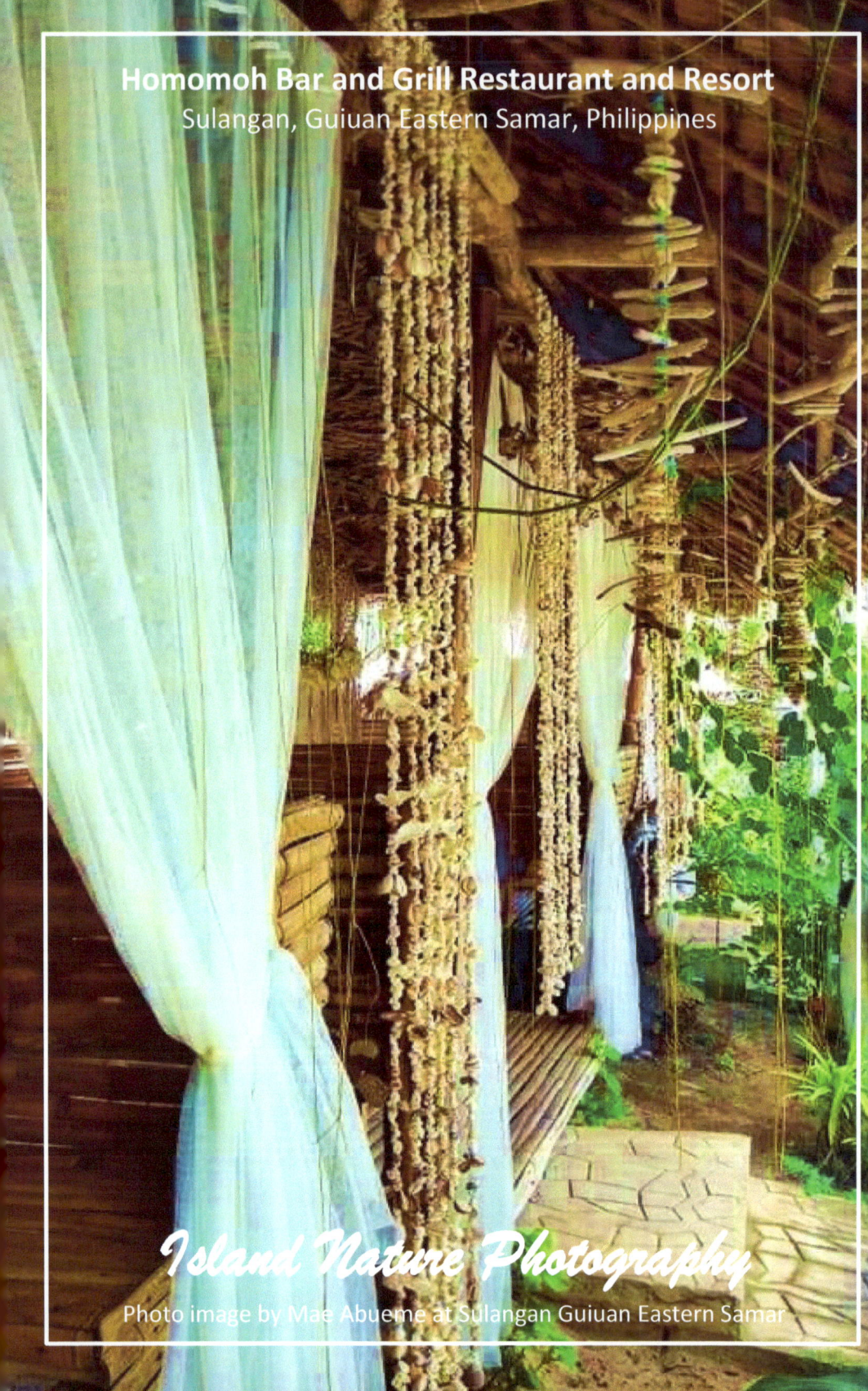

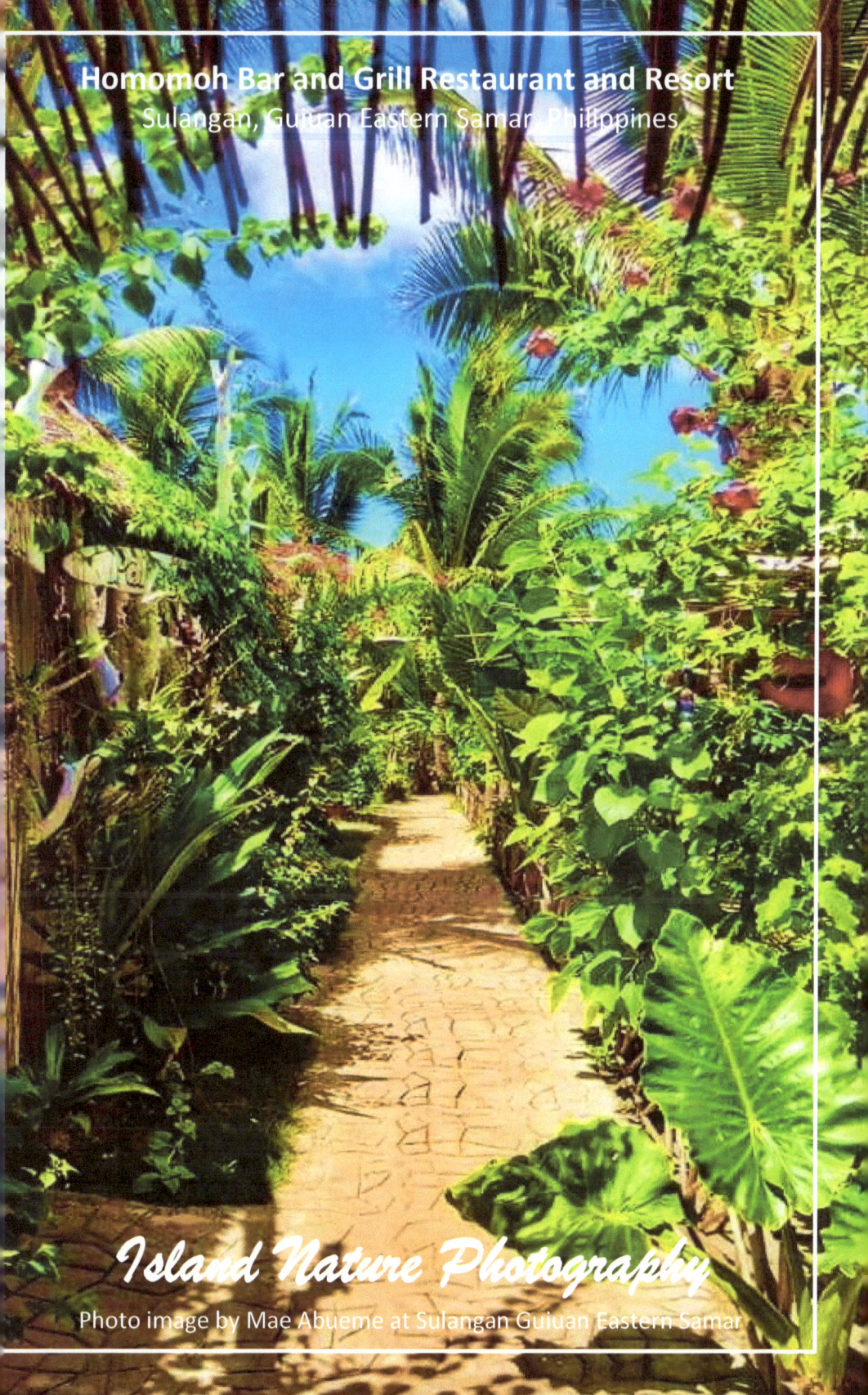

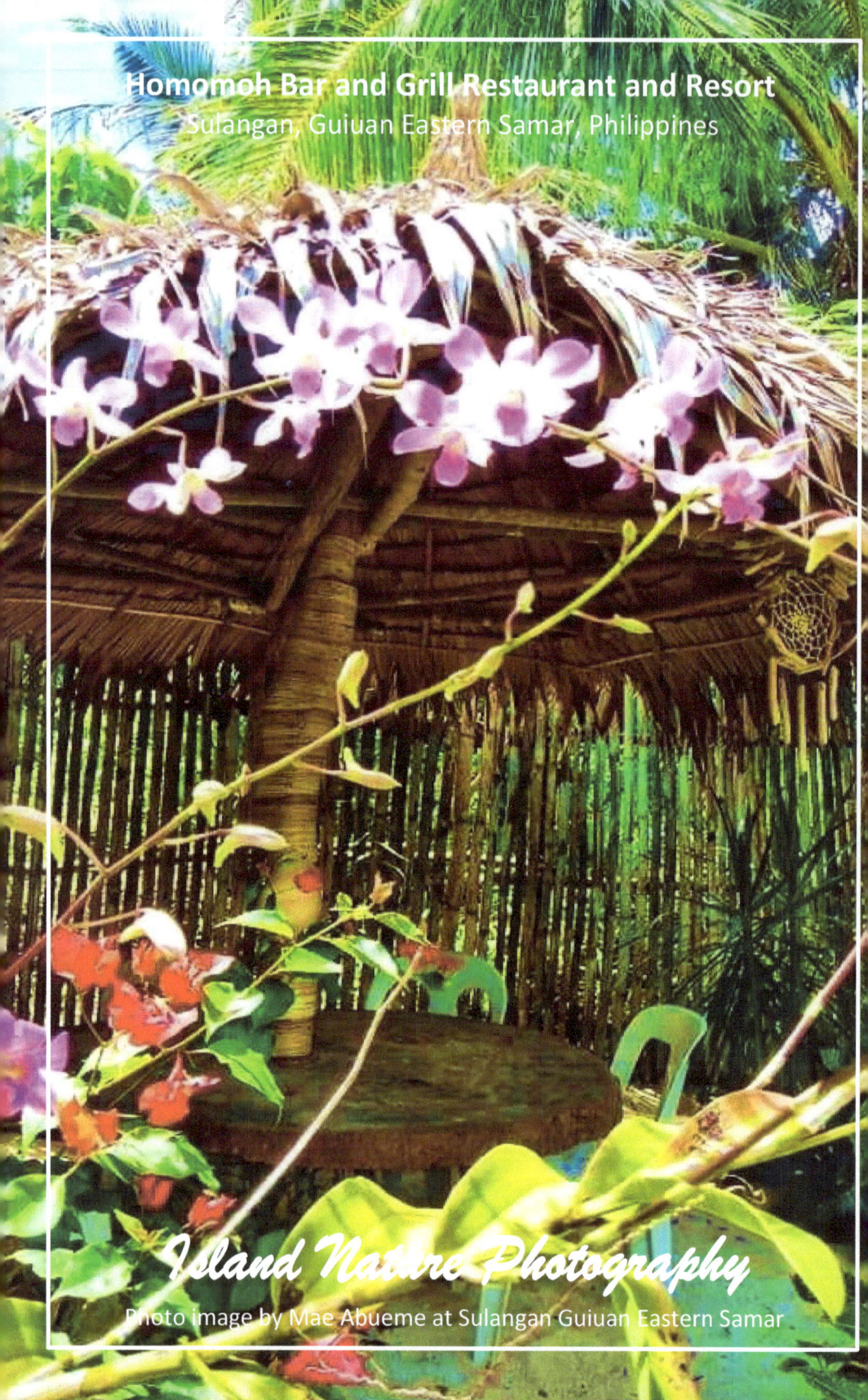

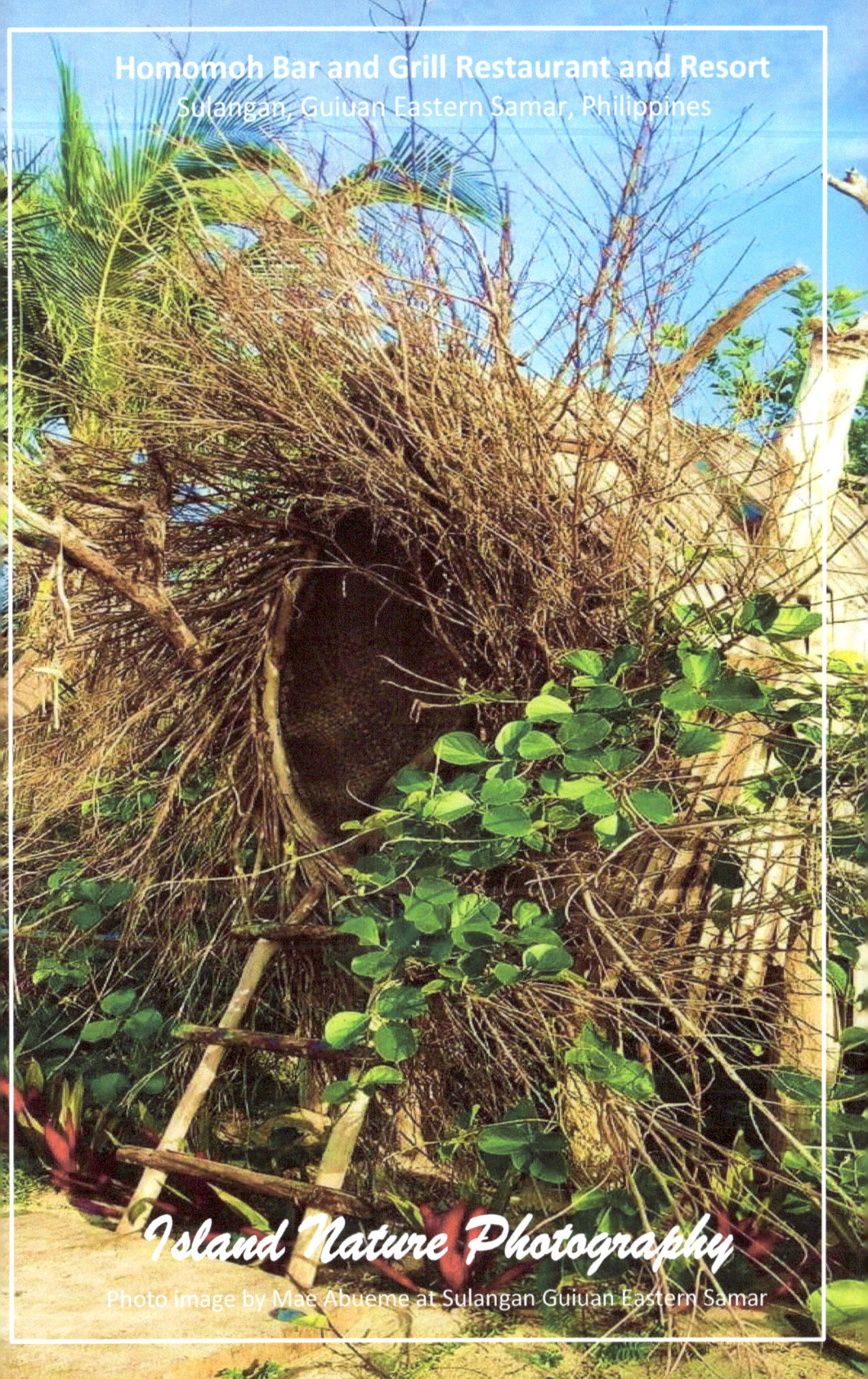

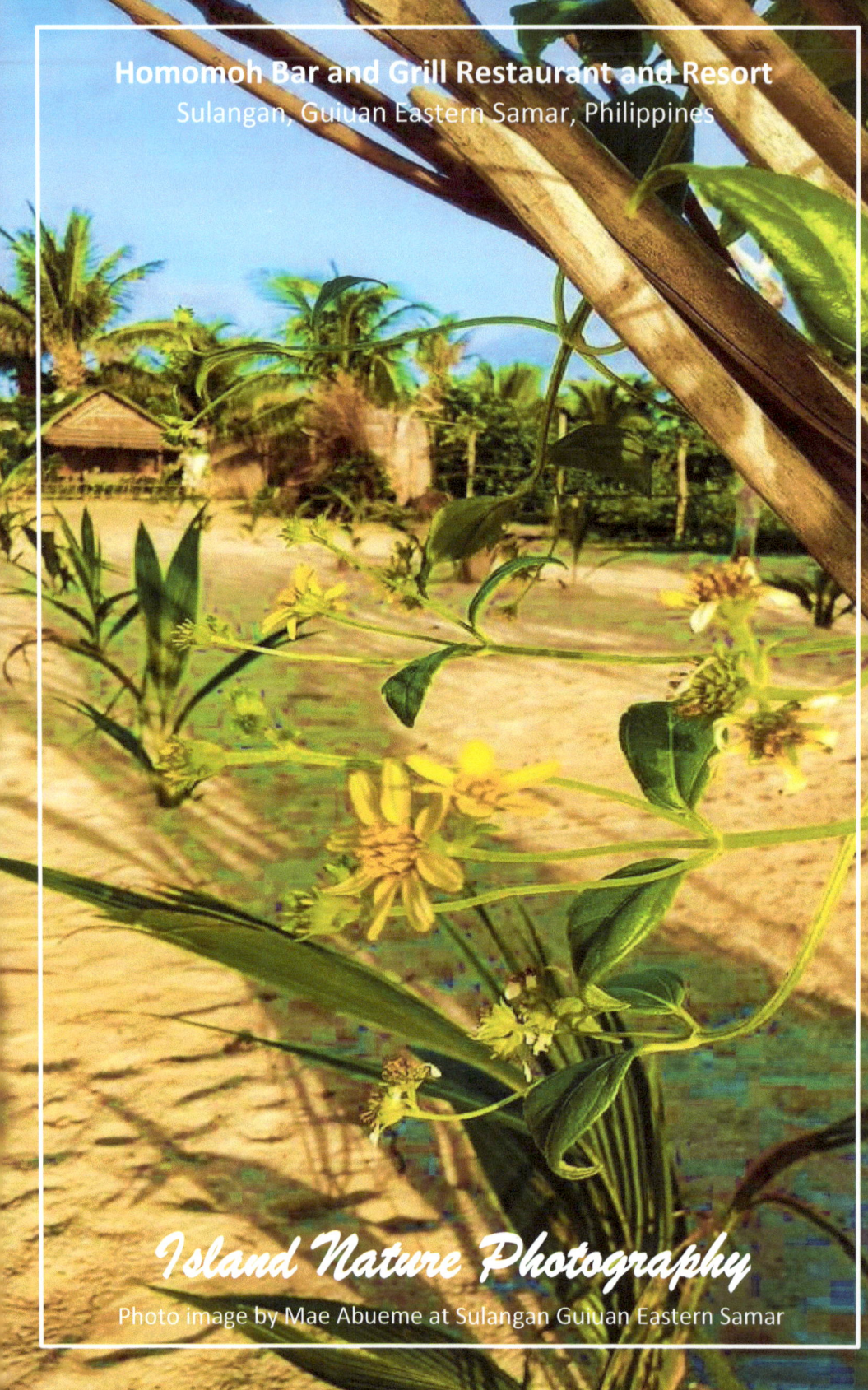

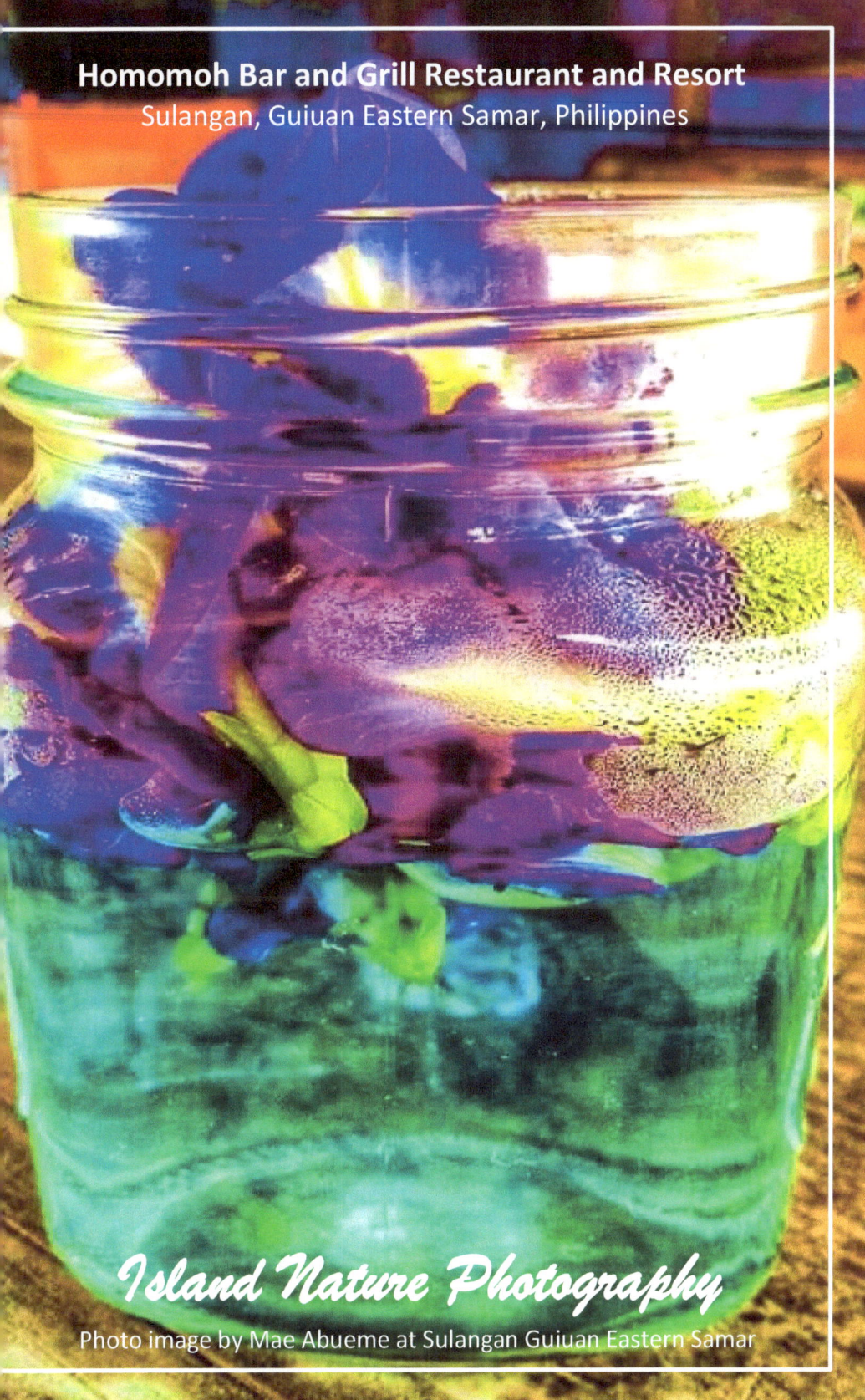

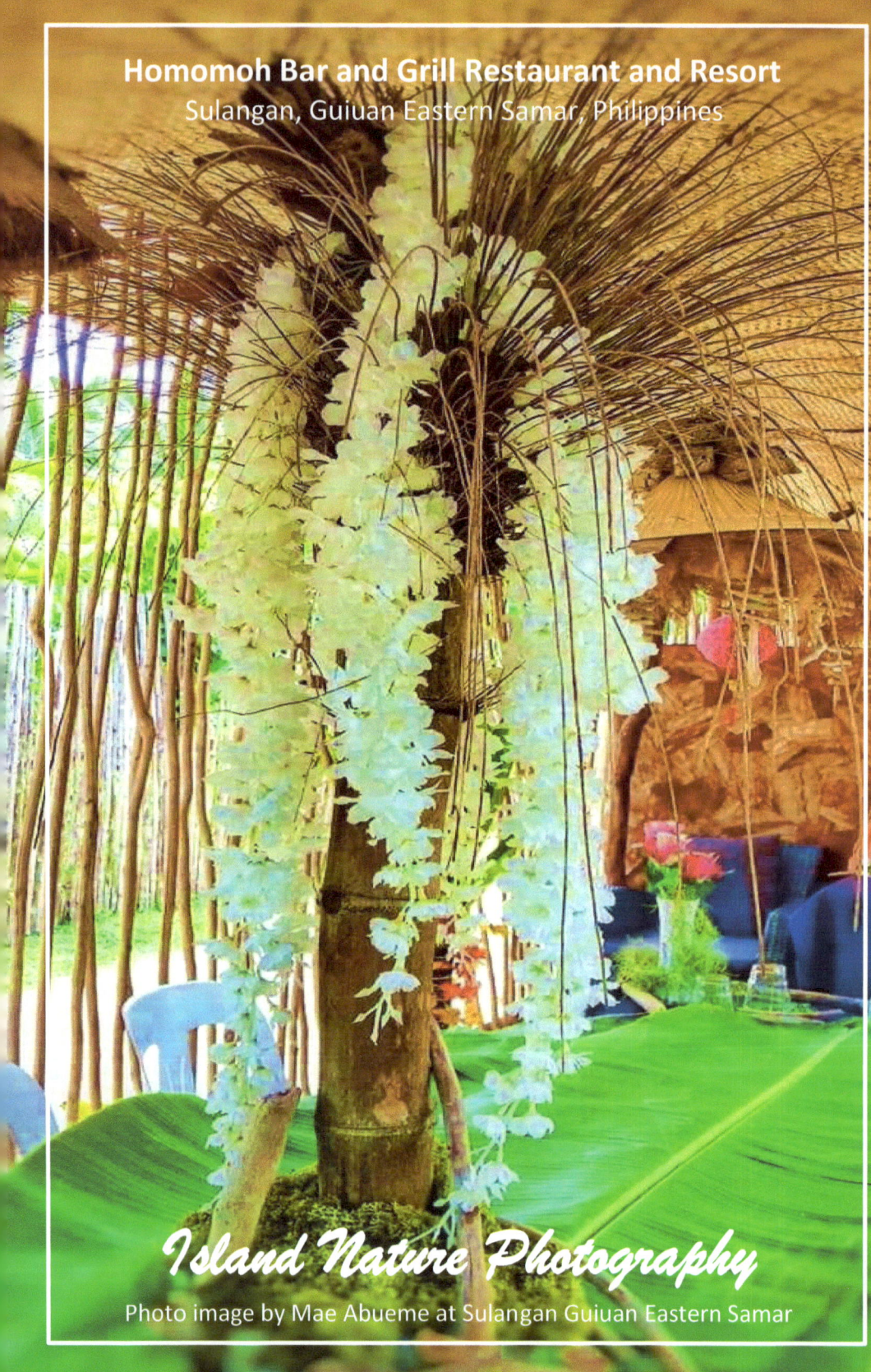

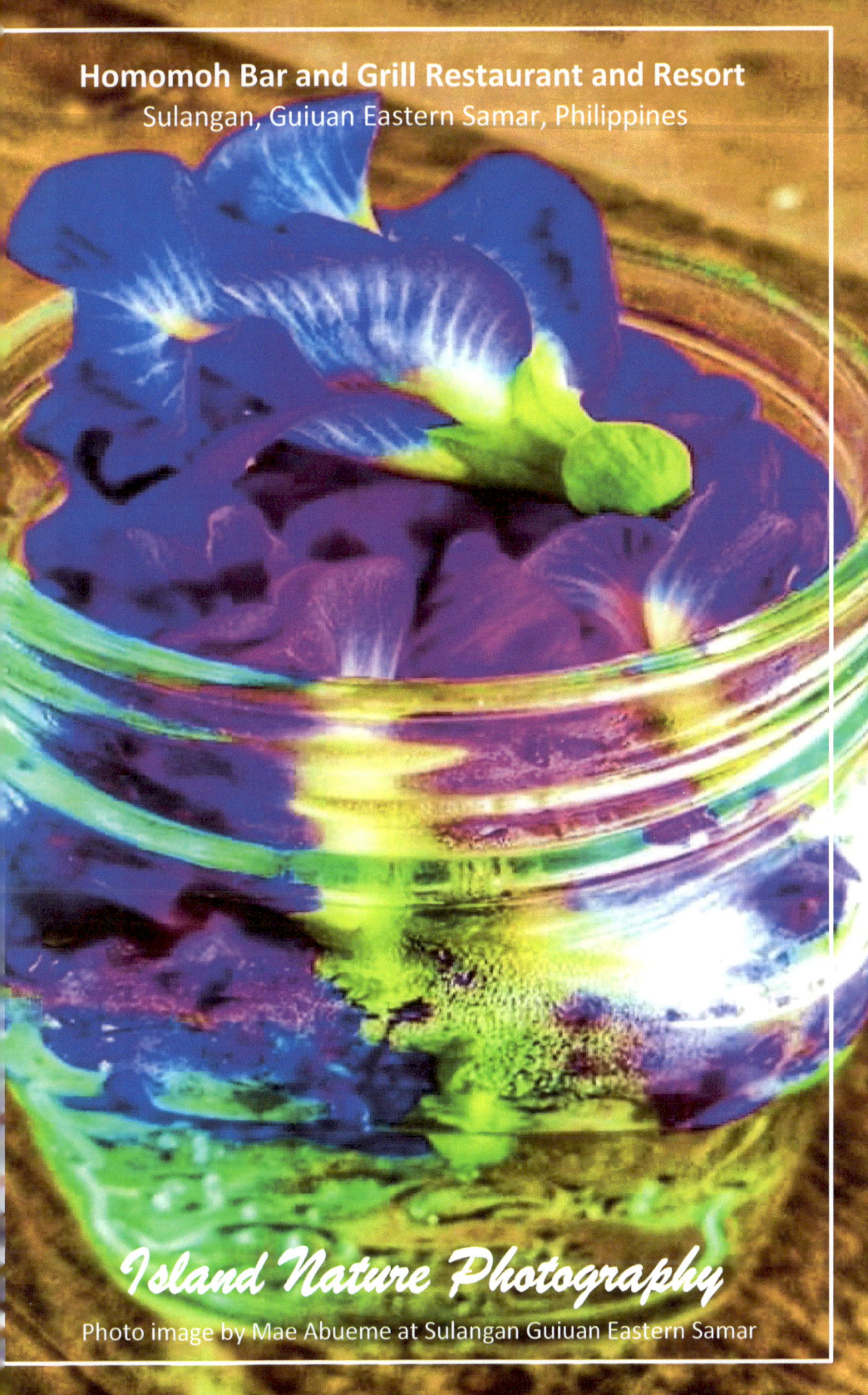

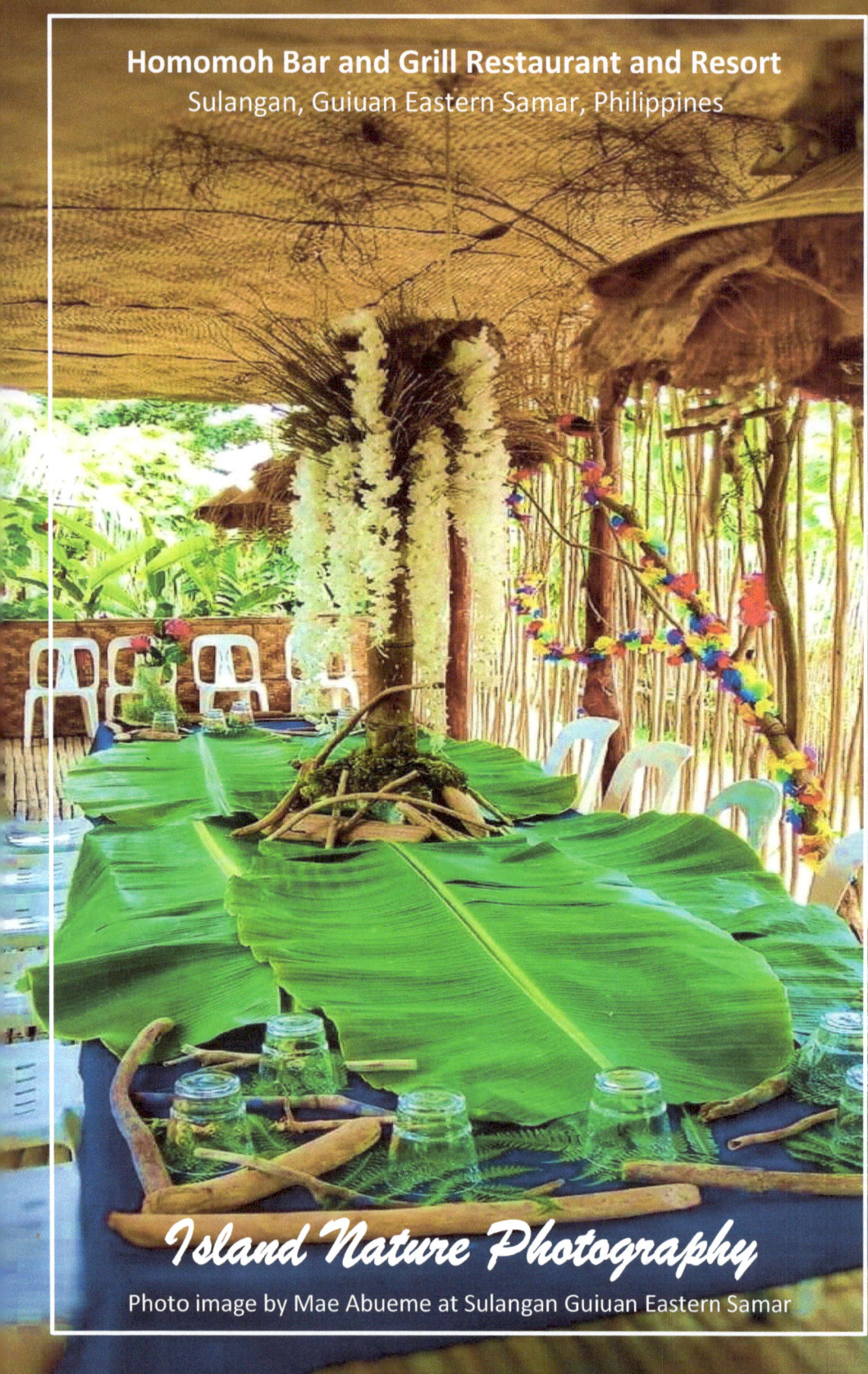

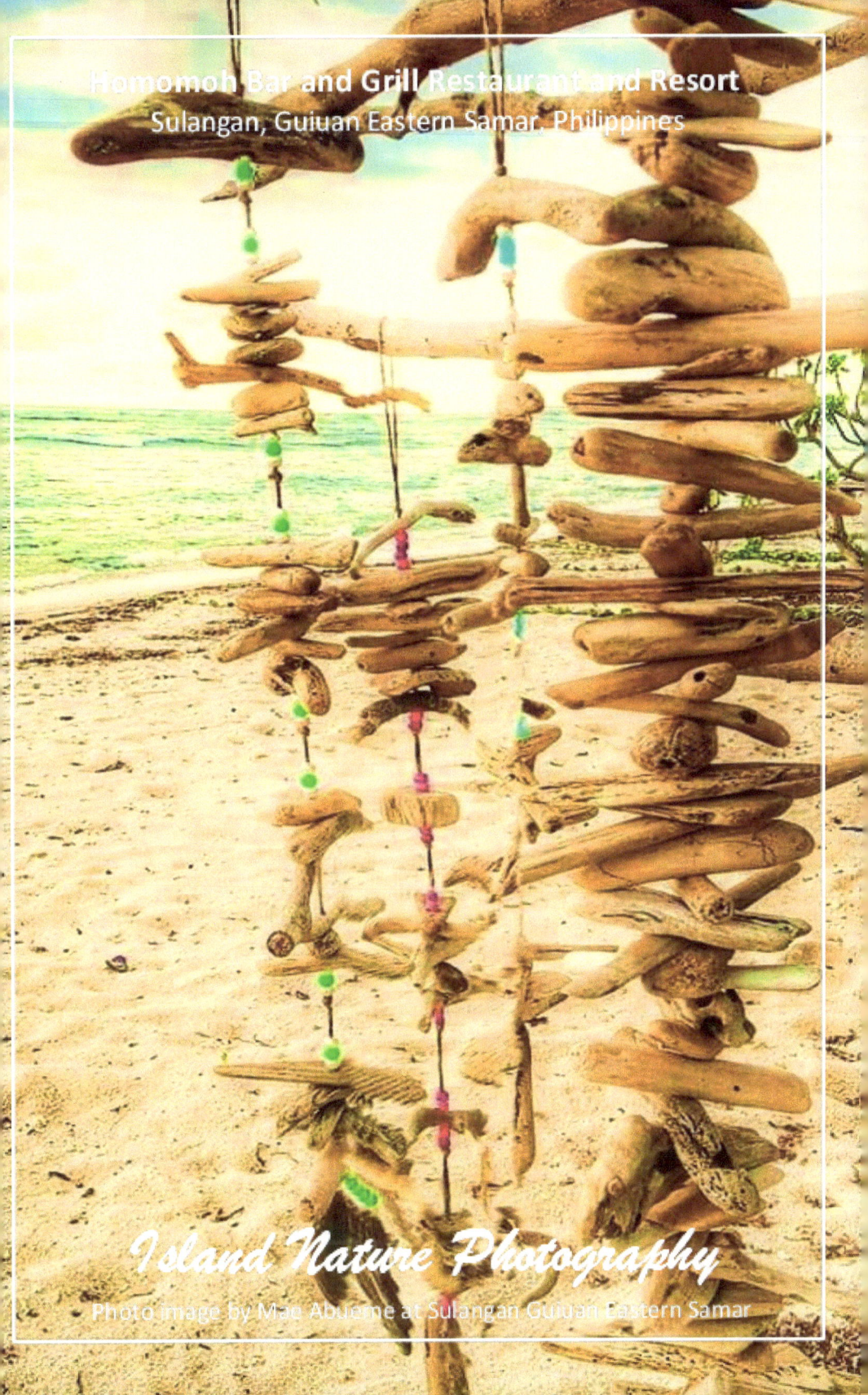

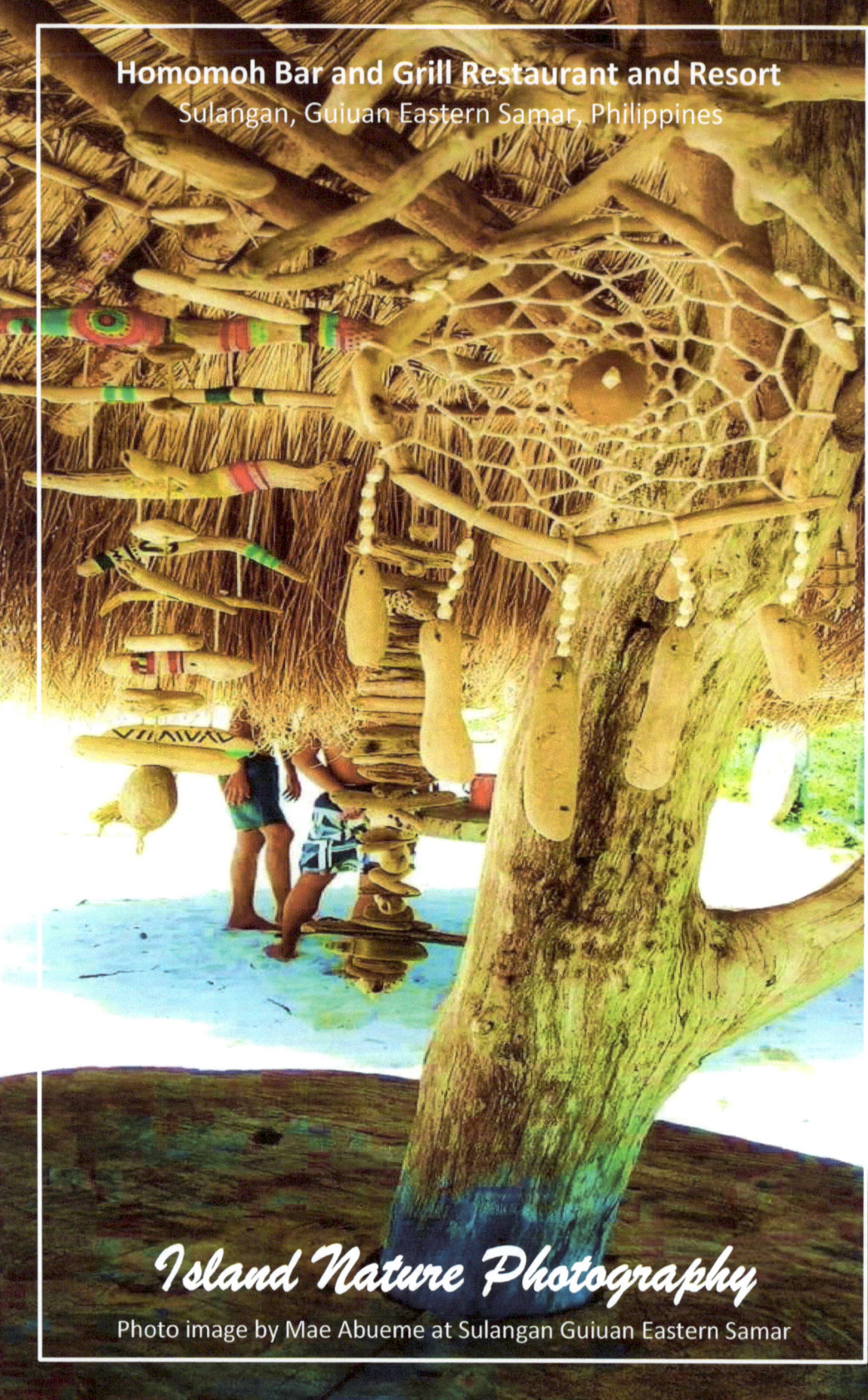

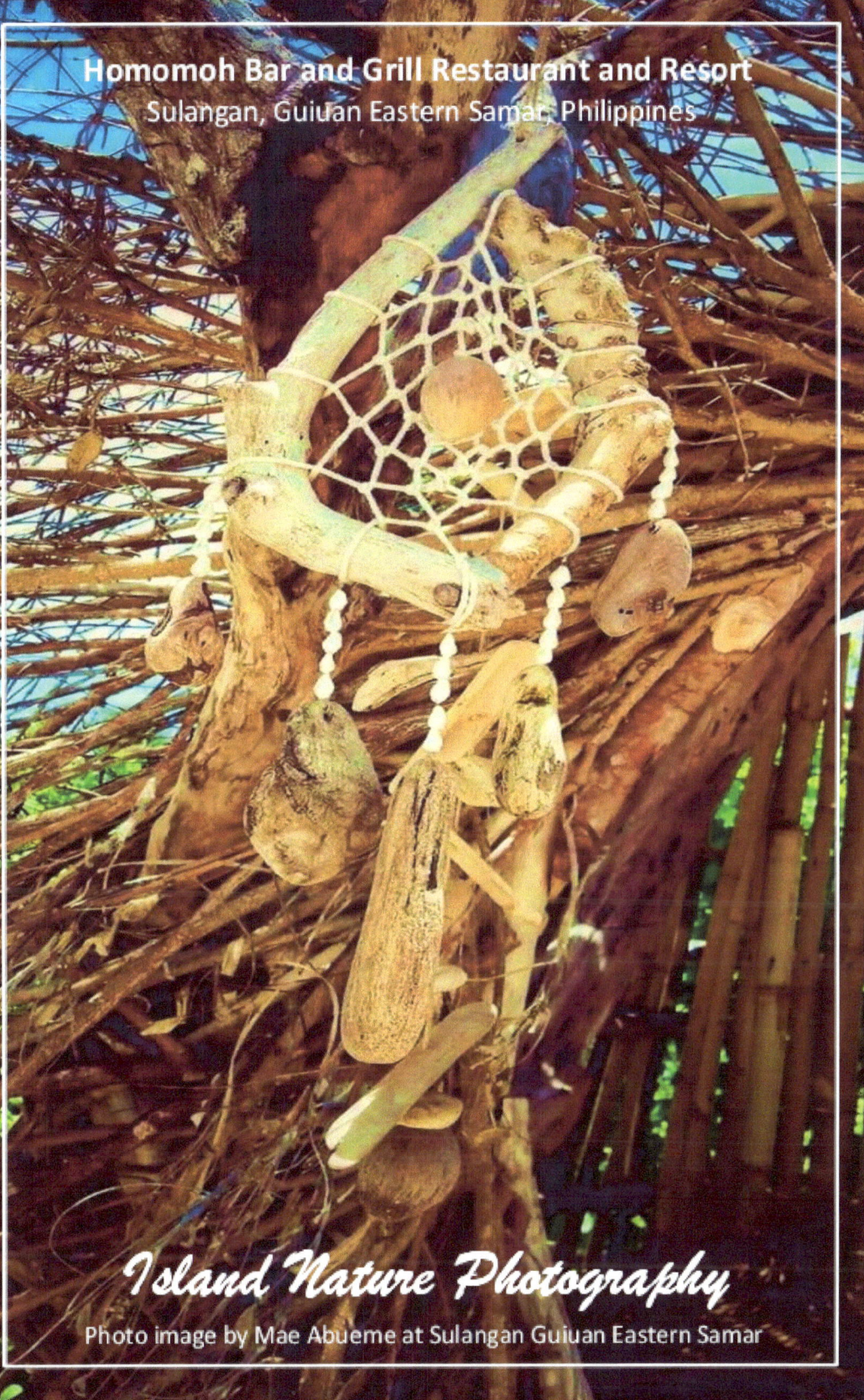

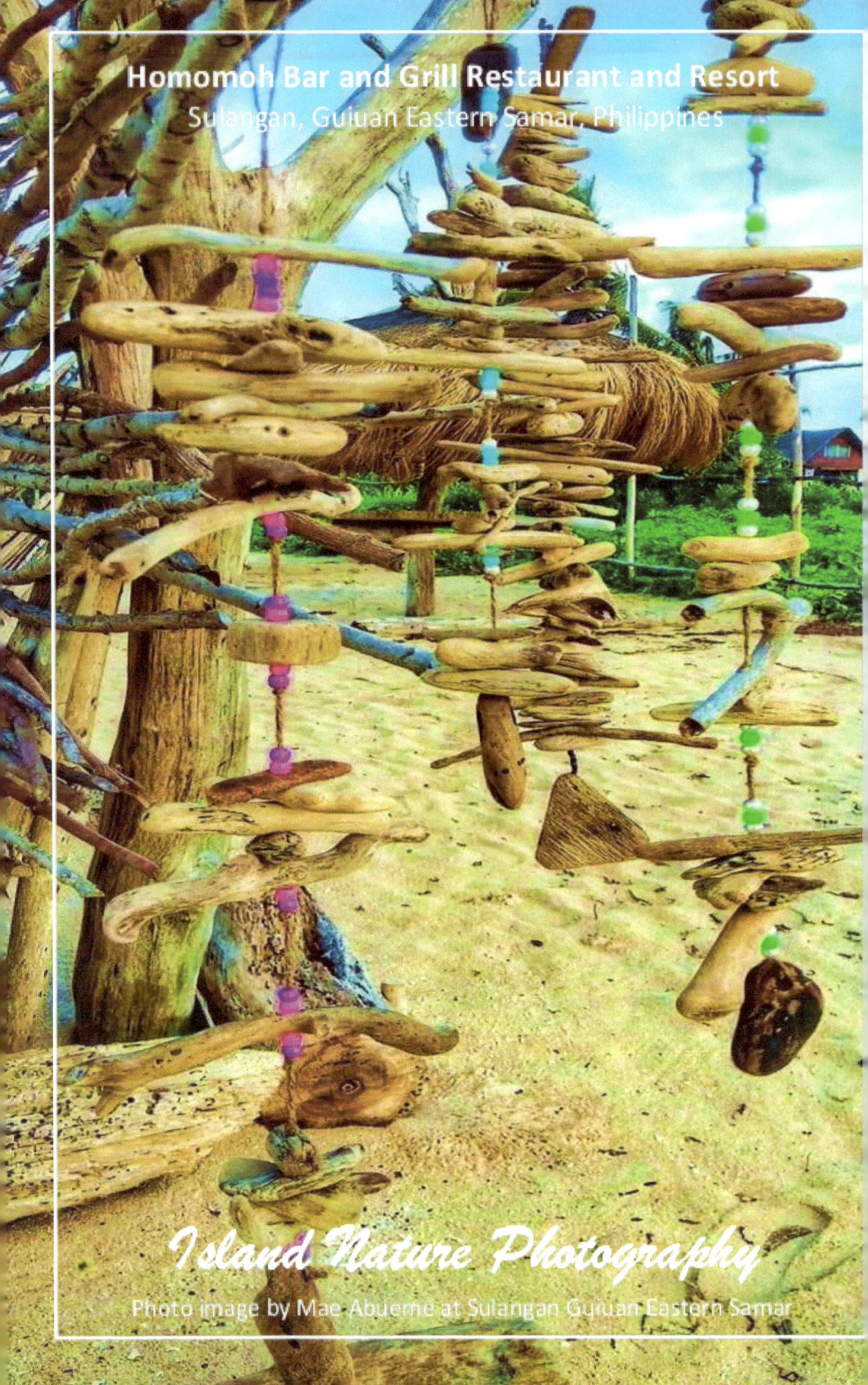

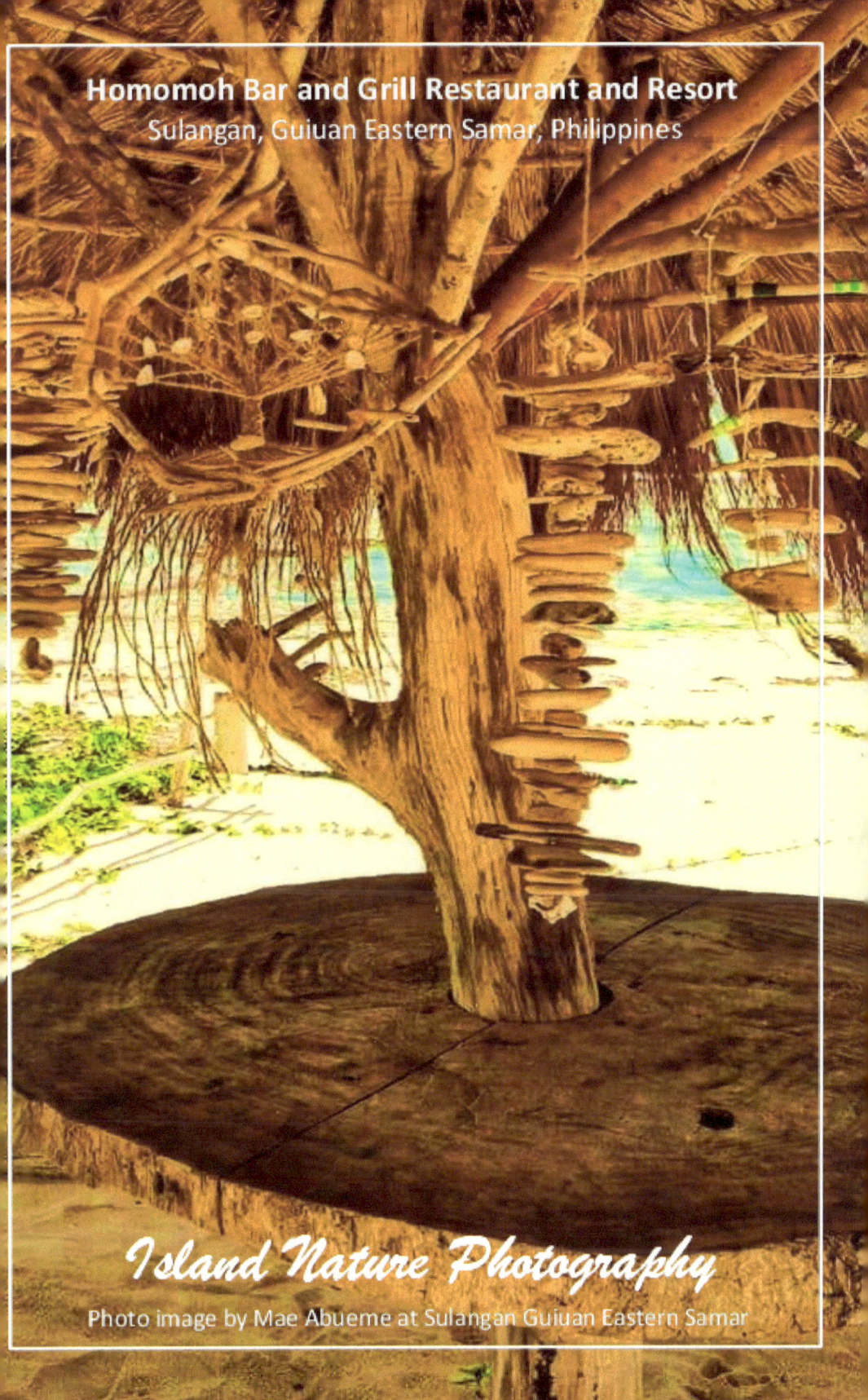

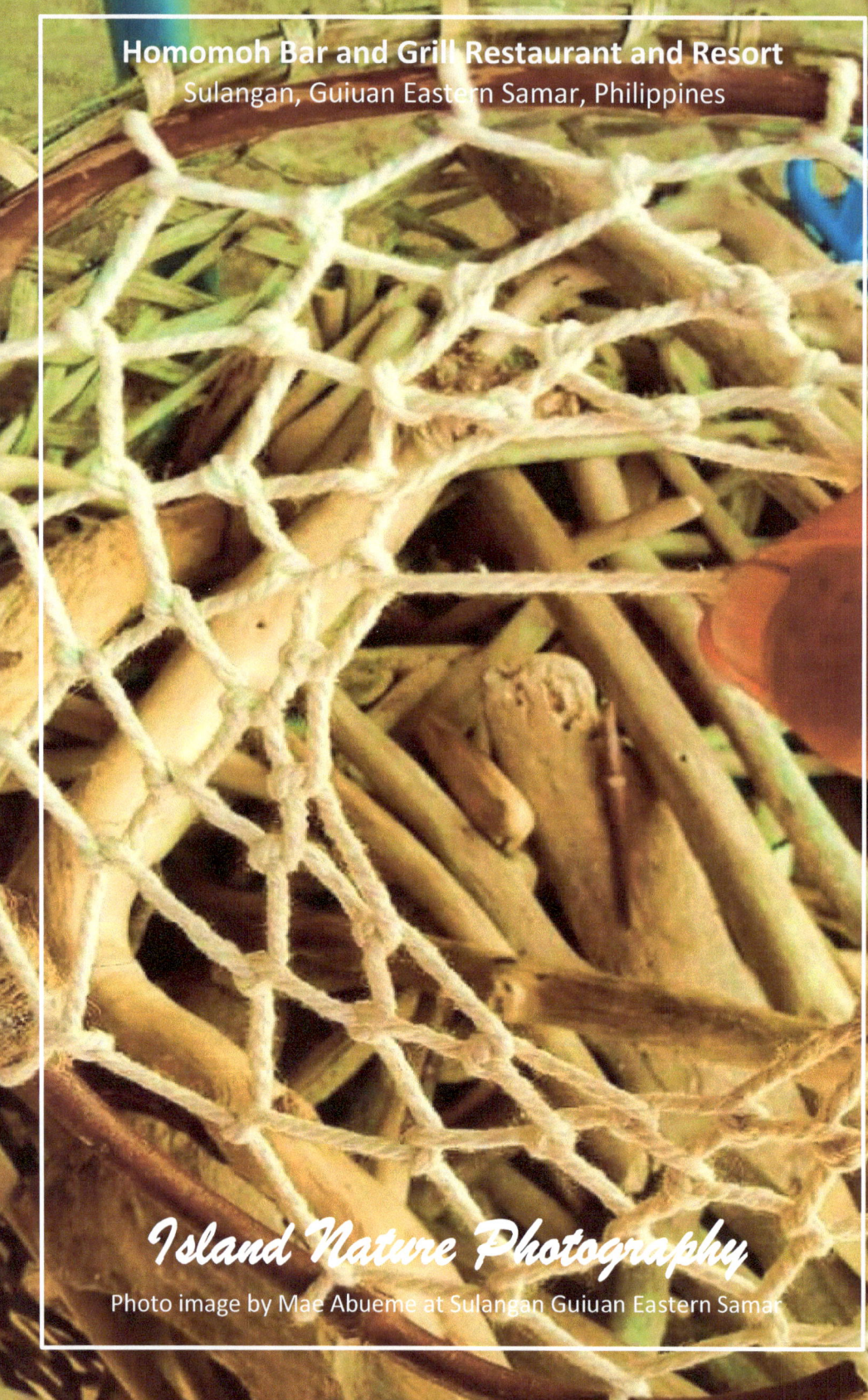

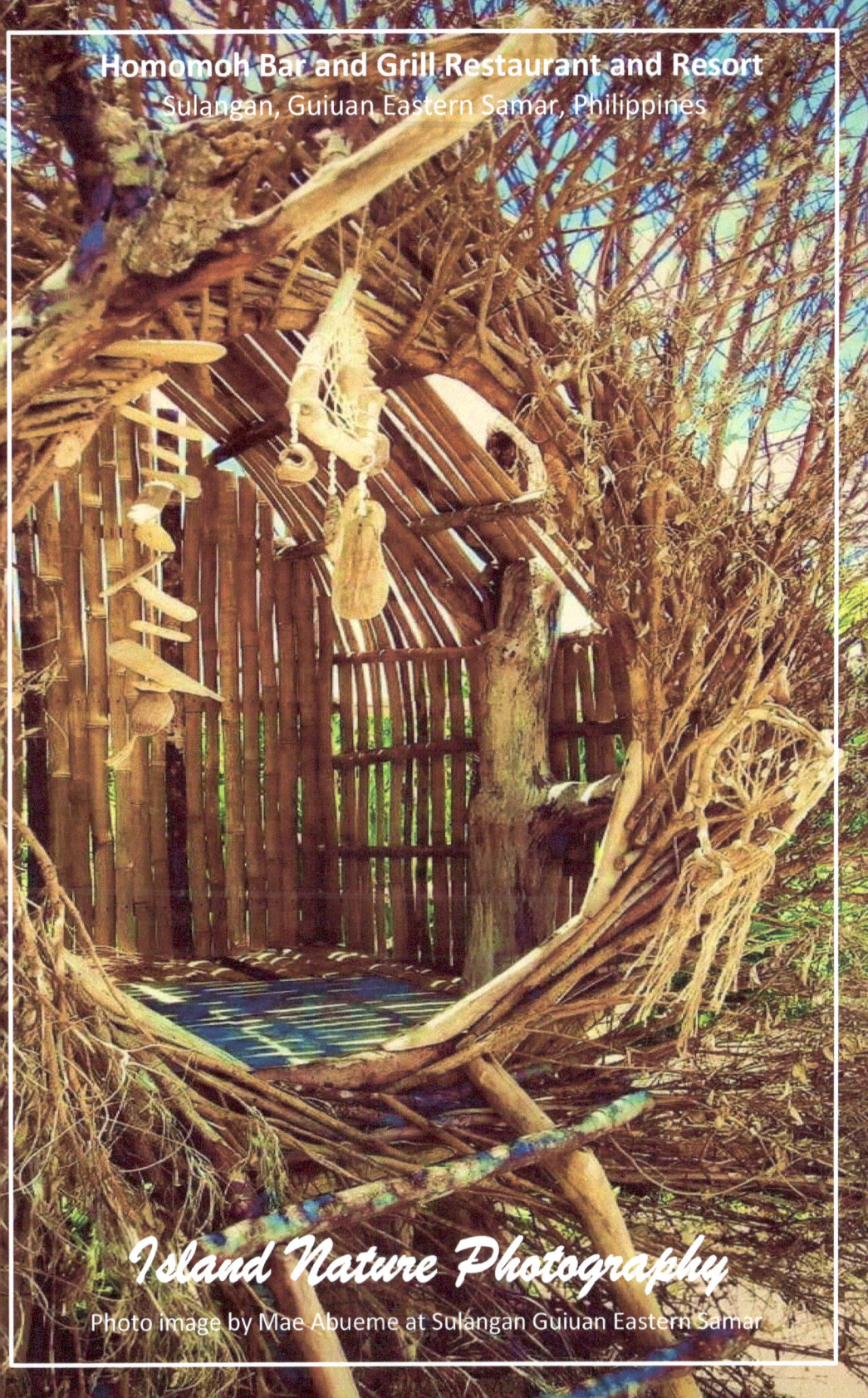

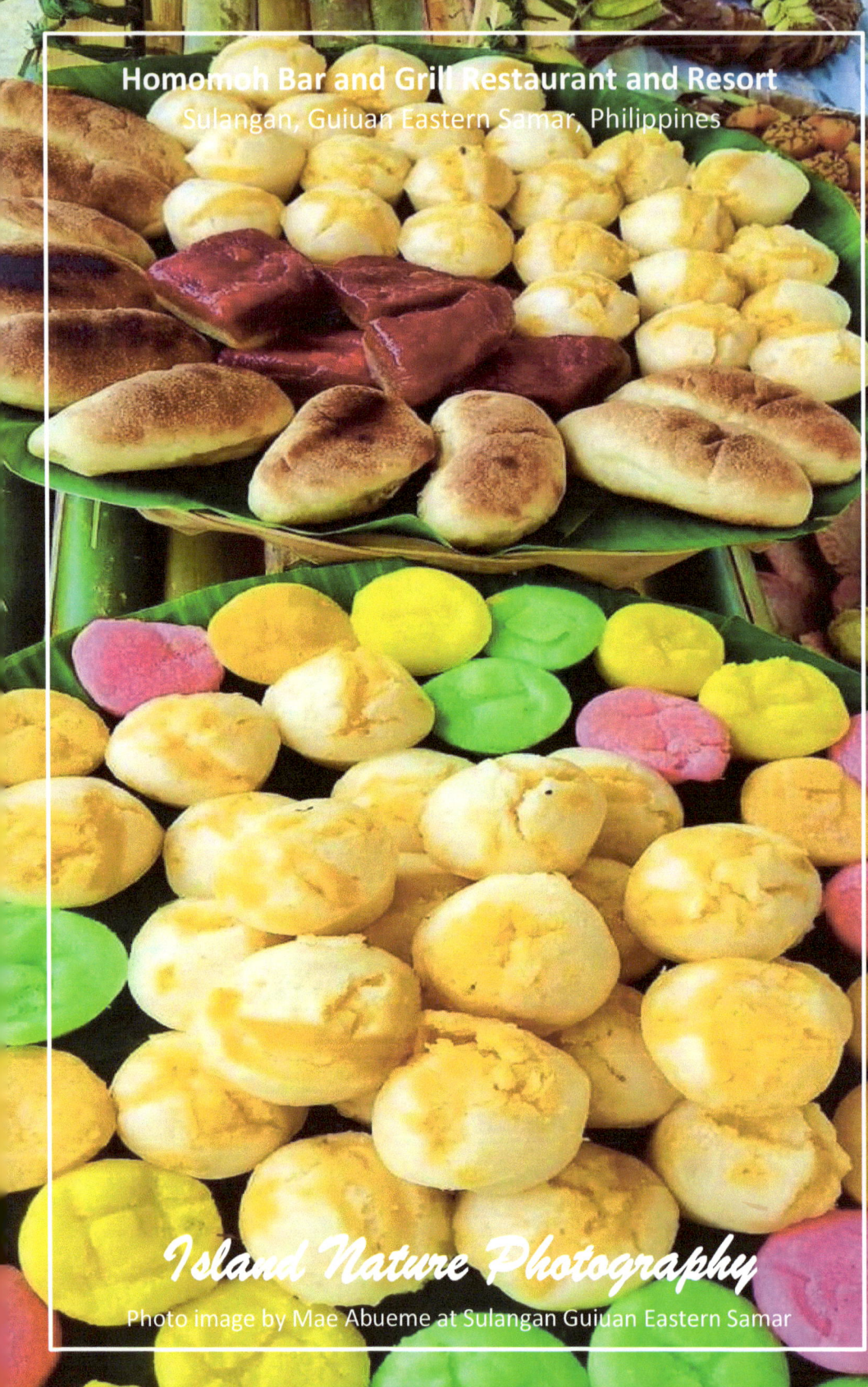

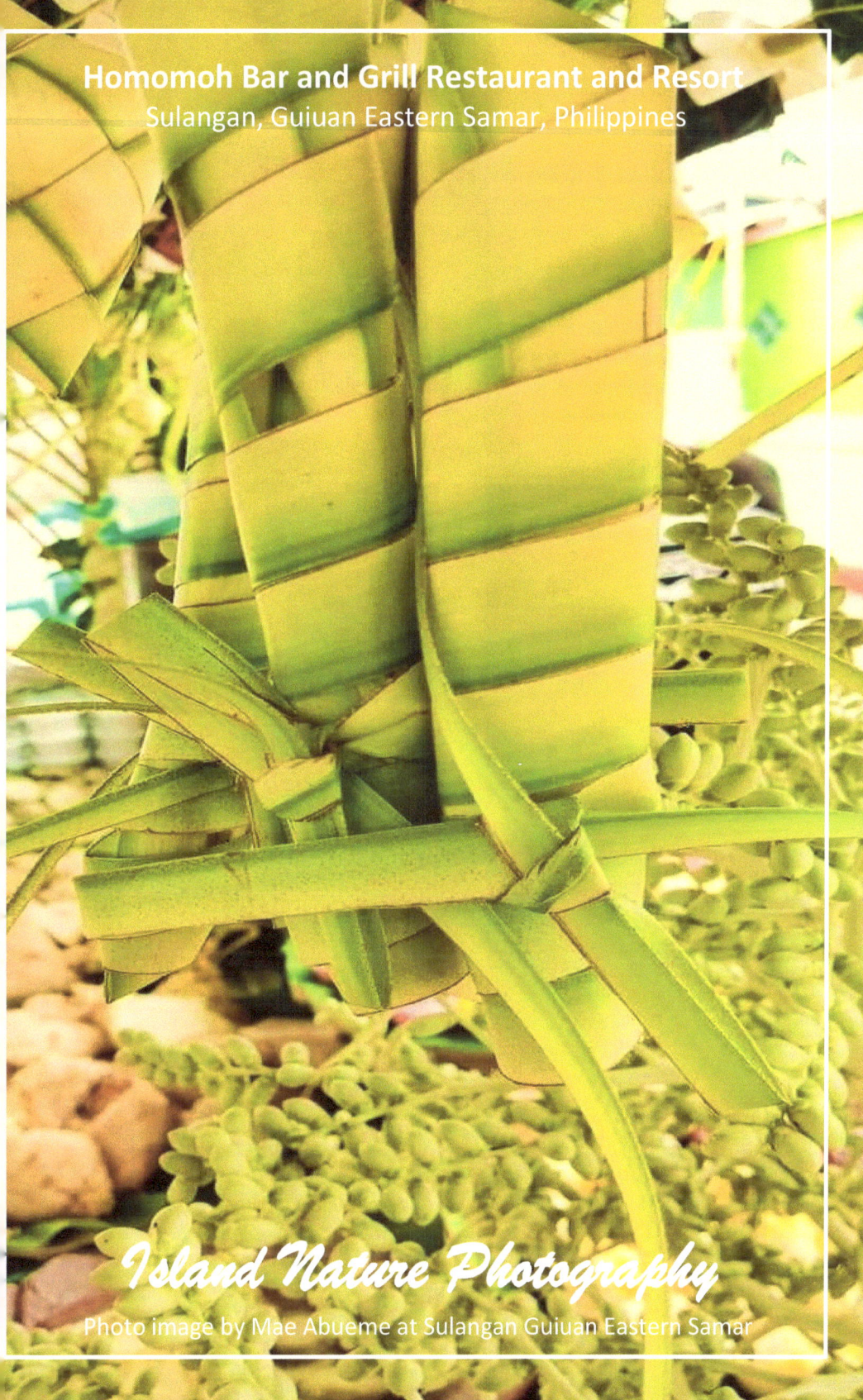

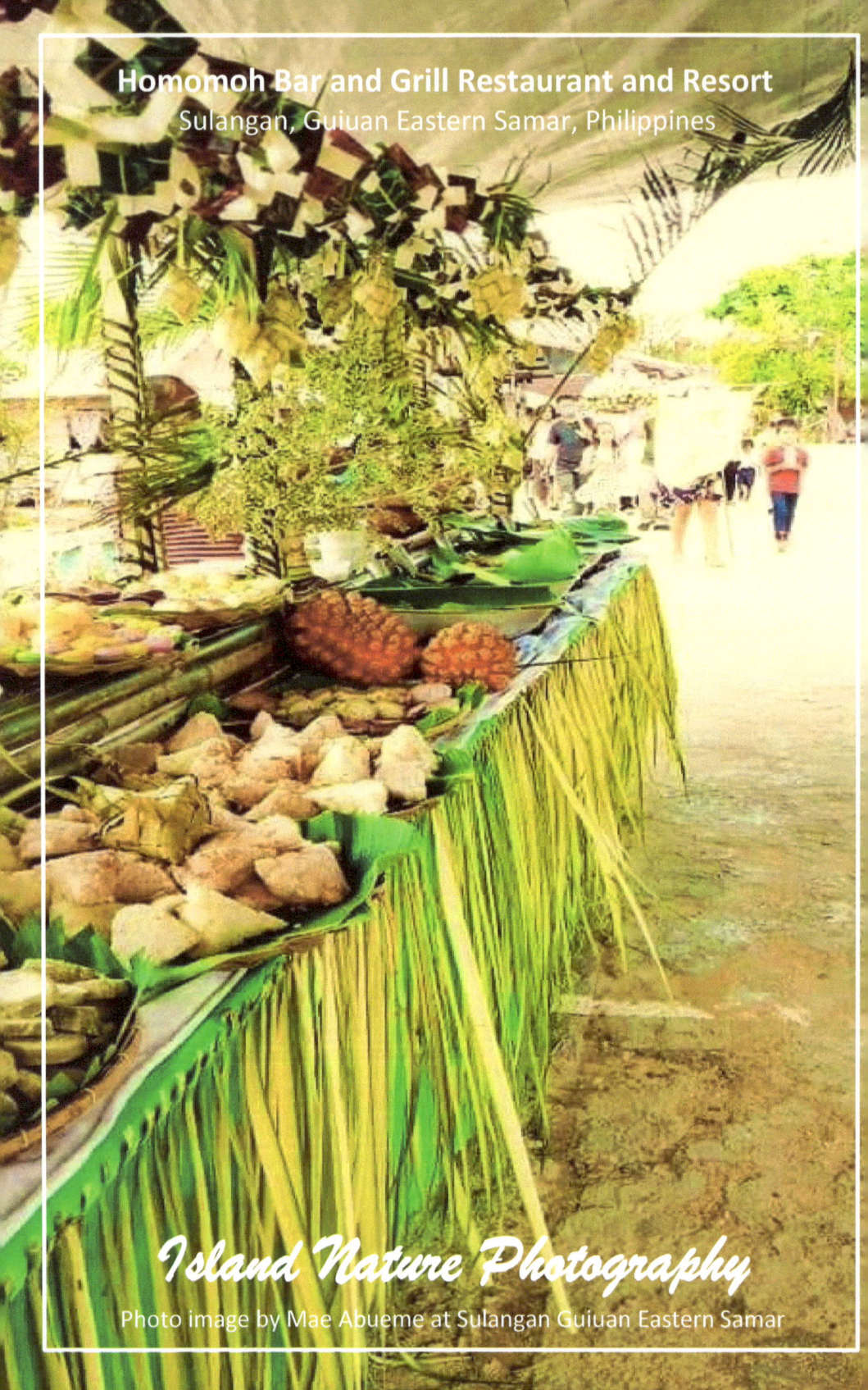

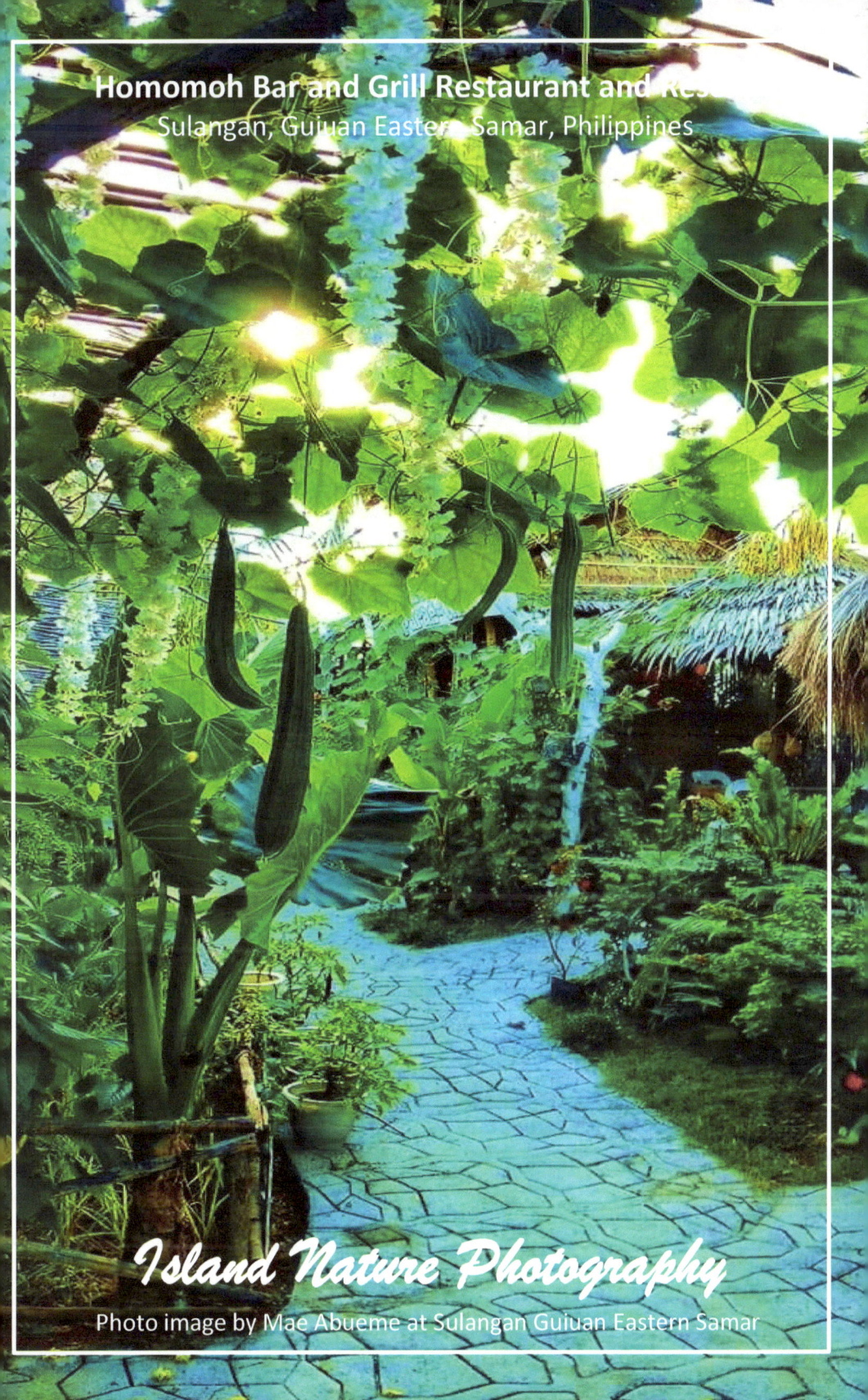

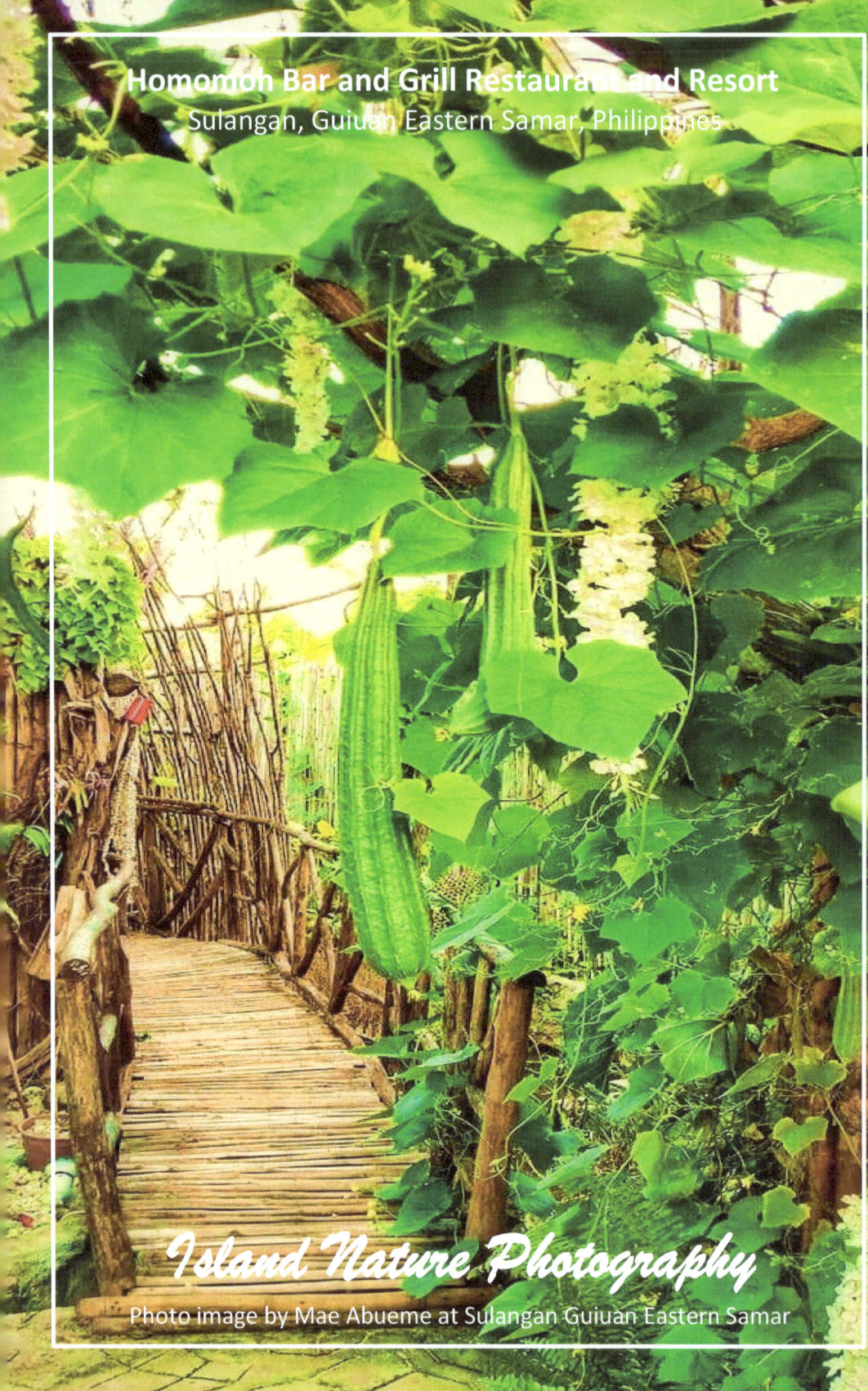

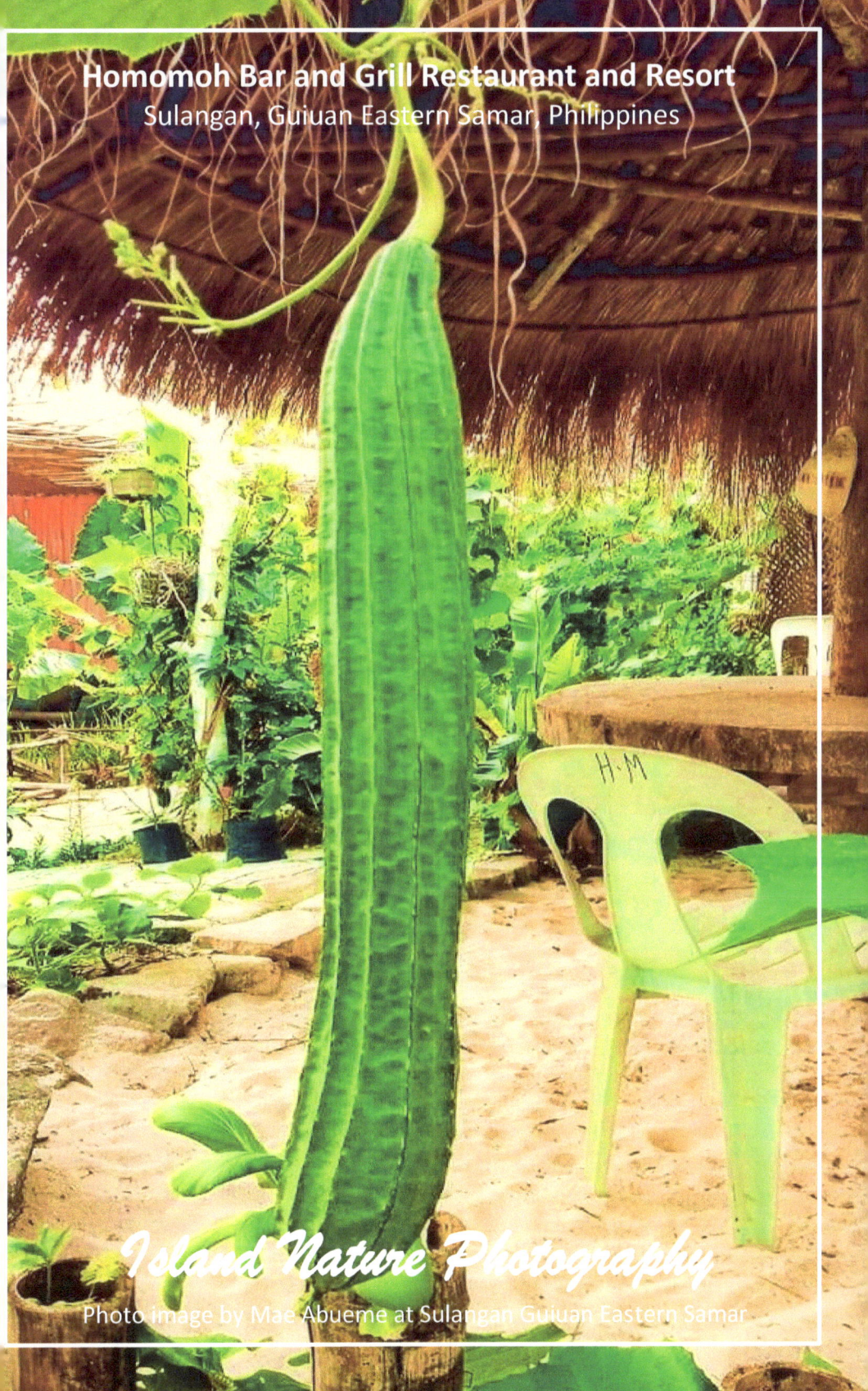

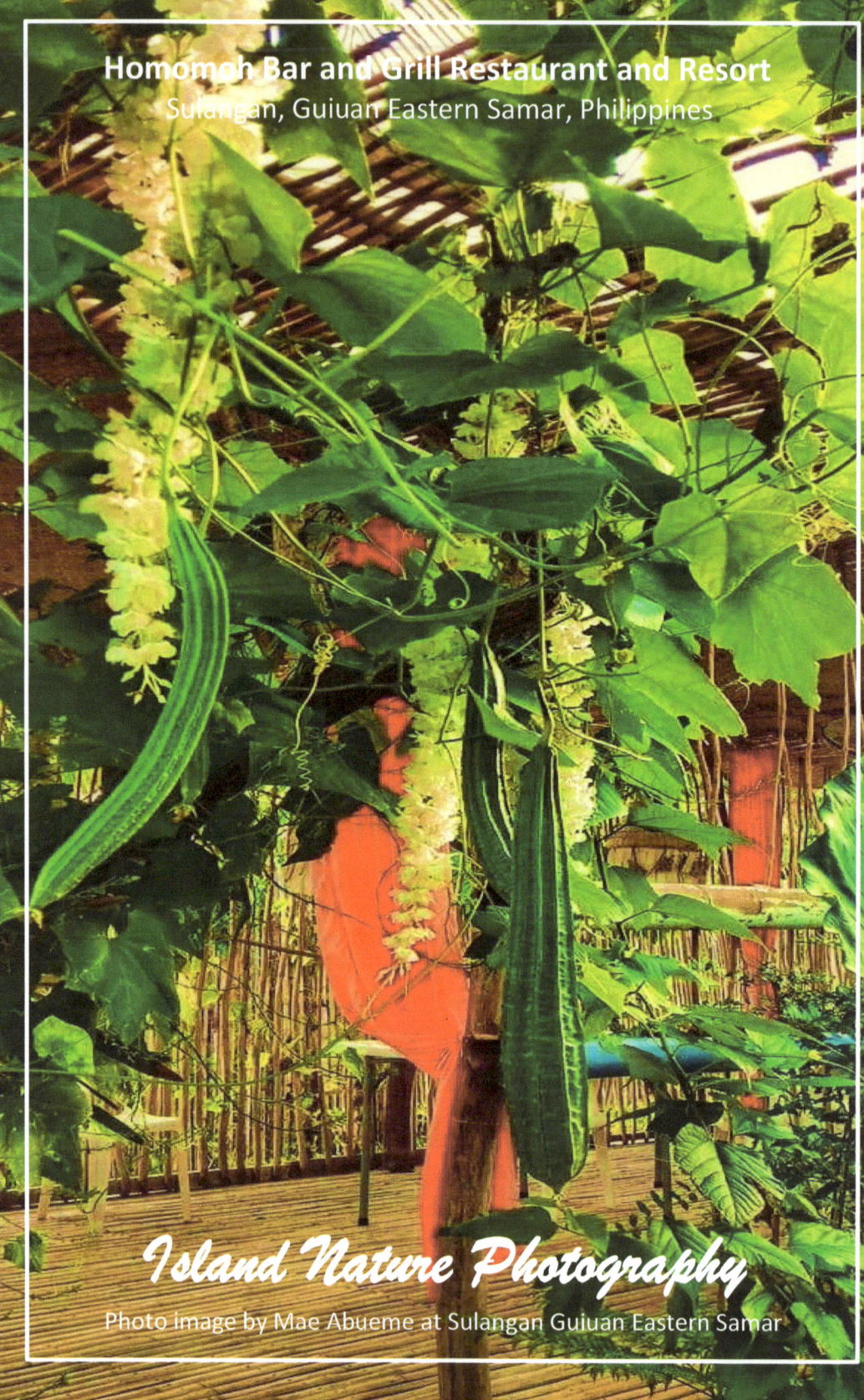

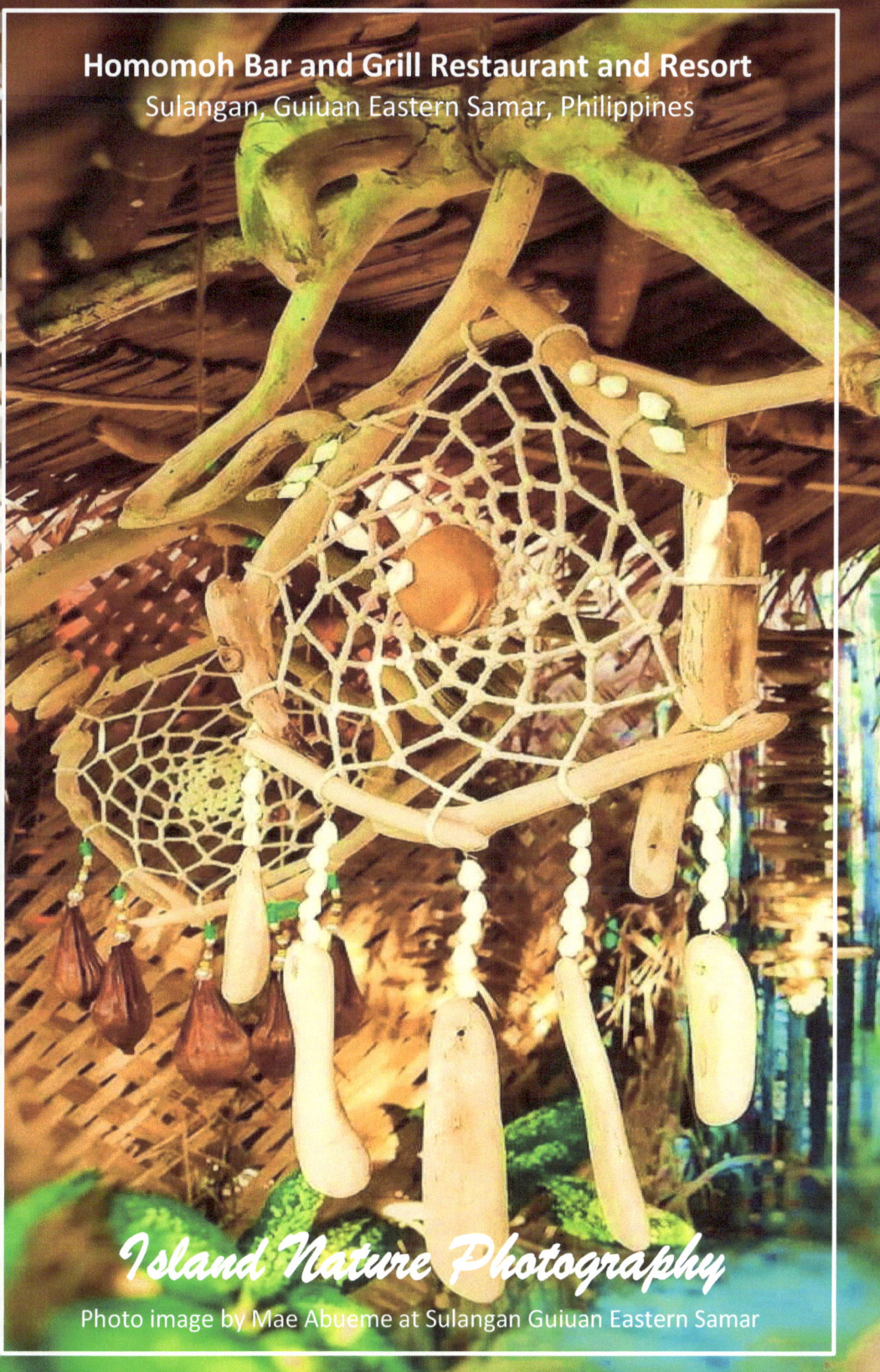

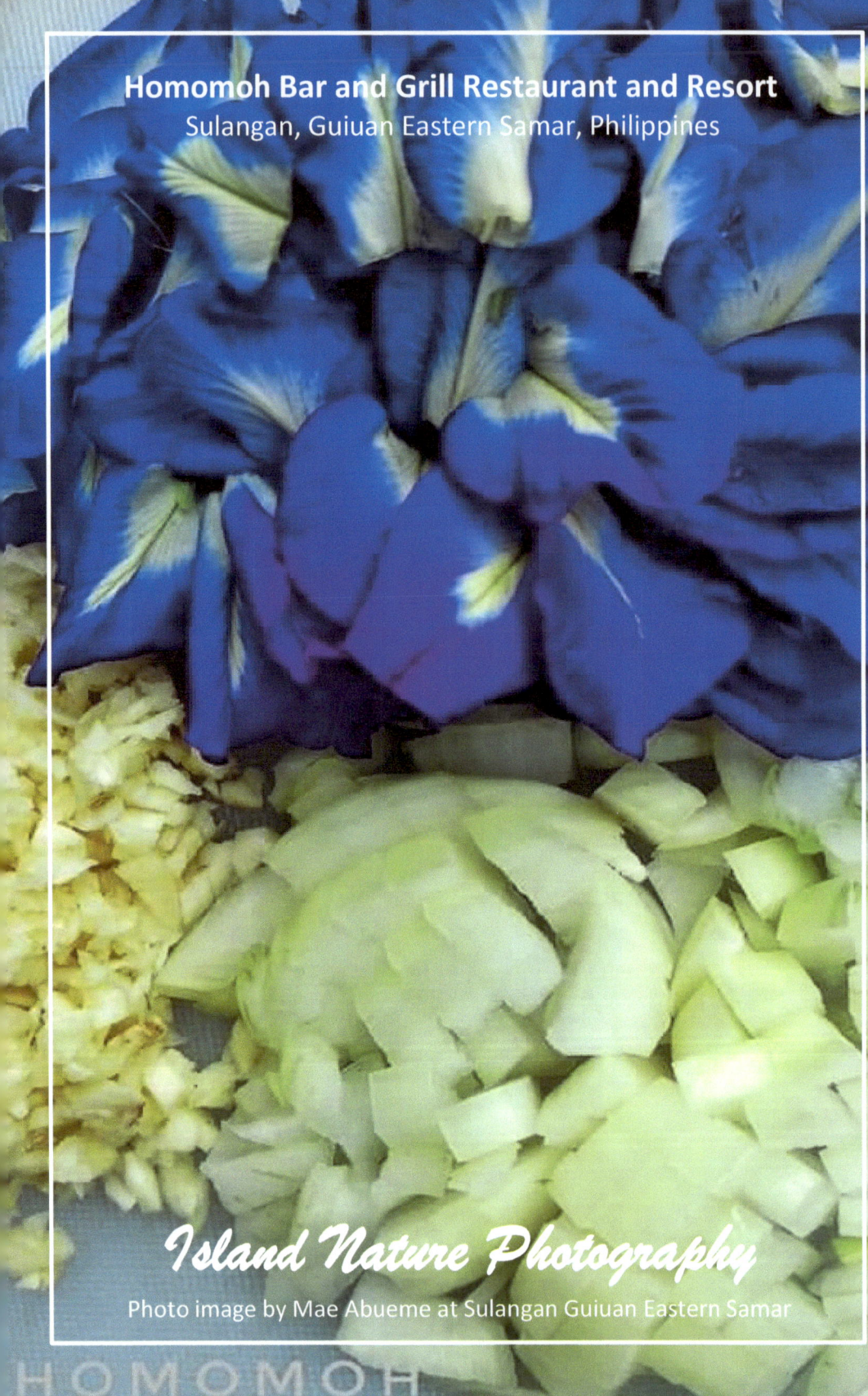

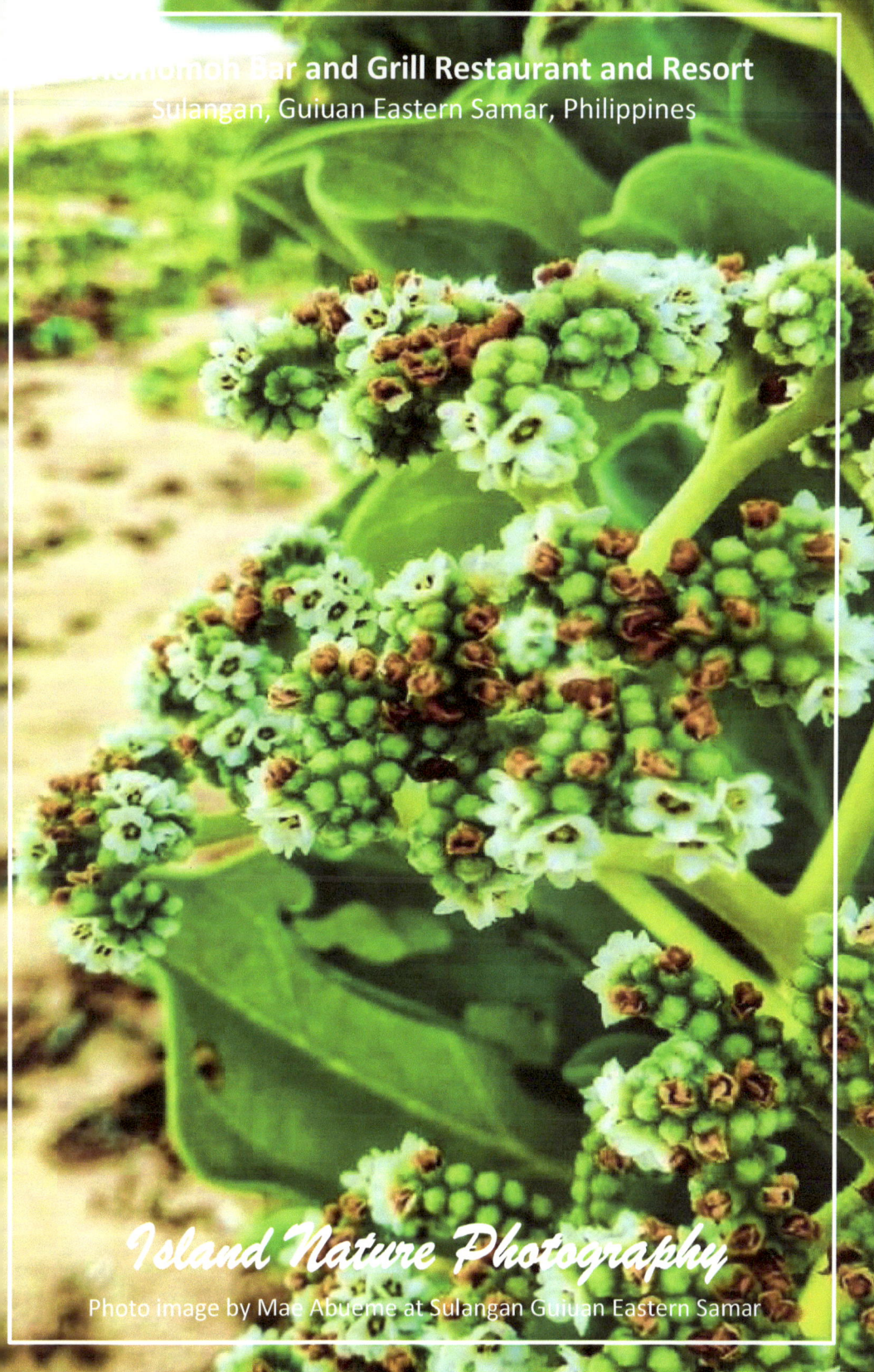

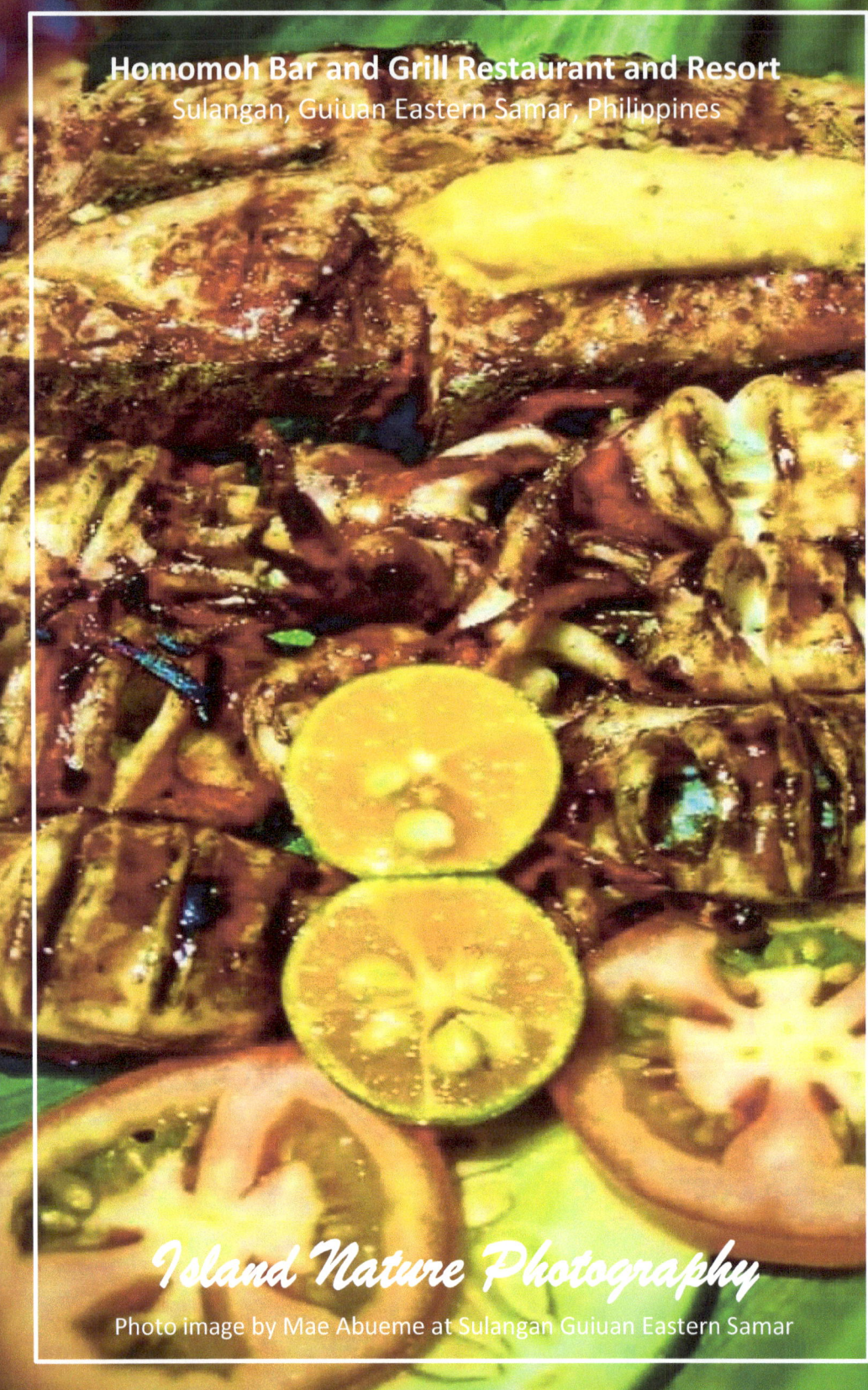

Homomoh Bar and Grill Restaurant and Resort
Sulangan, Guiuan Eastern Samar, Philippines

Island Nature Photography
Photo image by Mae Abueme at Sulangan Guiuan Eastern Samar

Homomoh Bar and Grill Restaurant and Resort
Sulangan, Guiuan Eastern Samar, Philippines

Island Nature Photography

Photo image by Mae Abueme at Sulangan Guiuan Eastern Samar

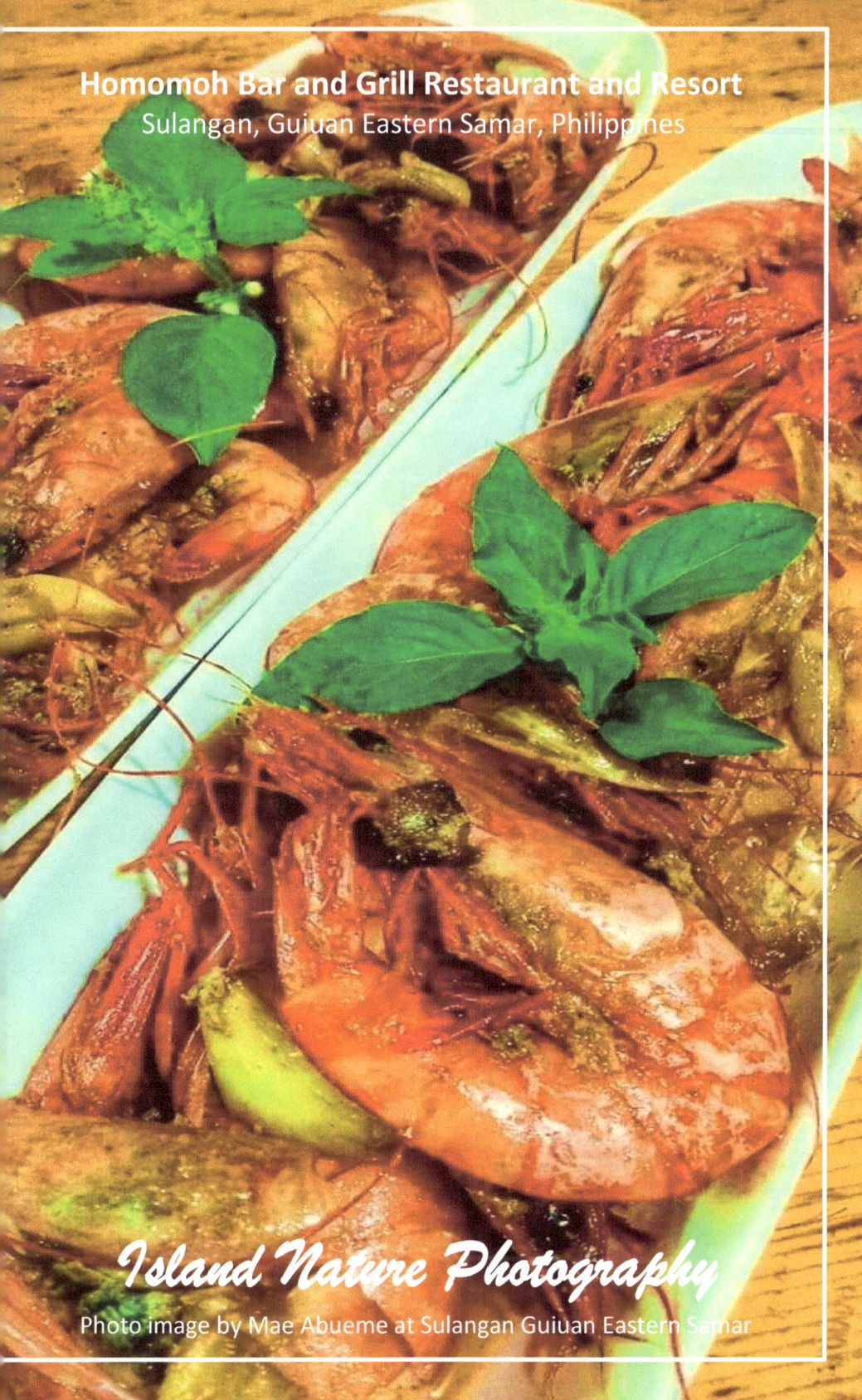

Homomoh Bar and Grill Restaurant and Resort
Sulangan, Guiuan Eastern Samar, Philippines

Island Nature Photography
Photo image by Mae Abueme at Sulangan Guiuan Eastern Samar

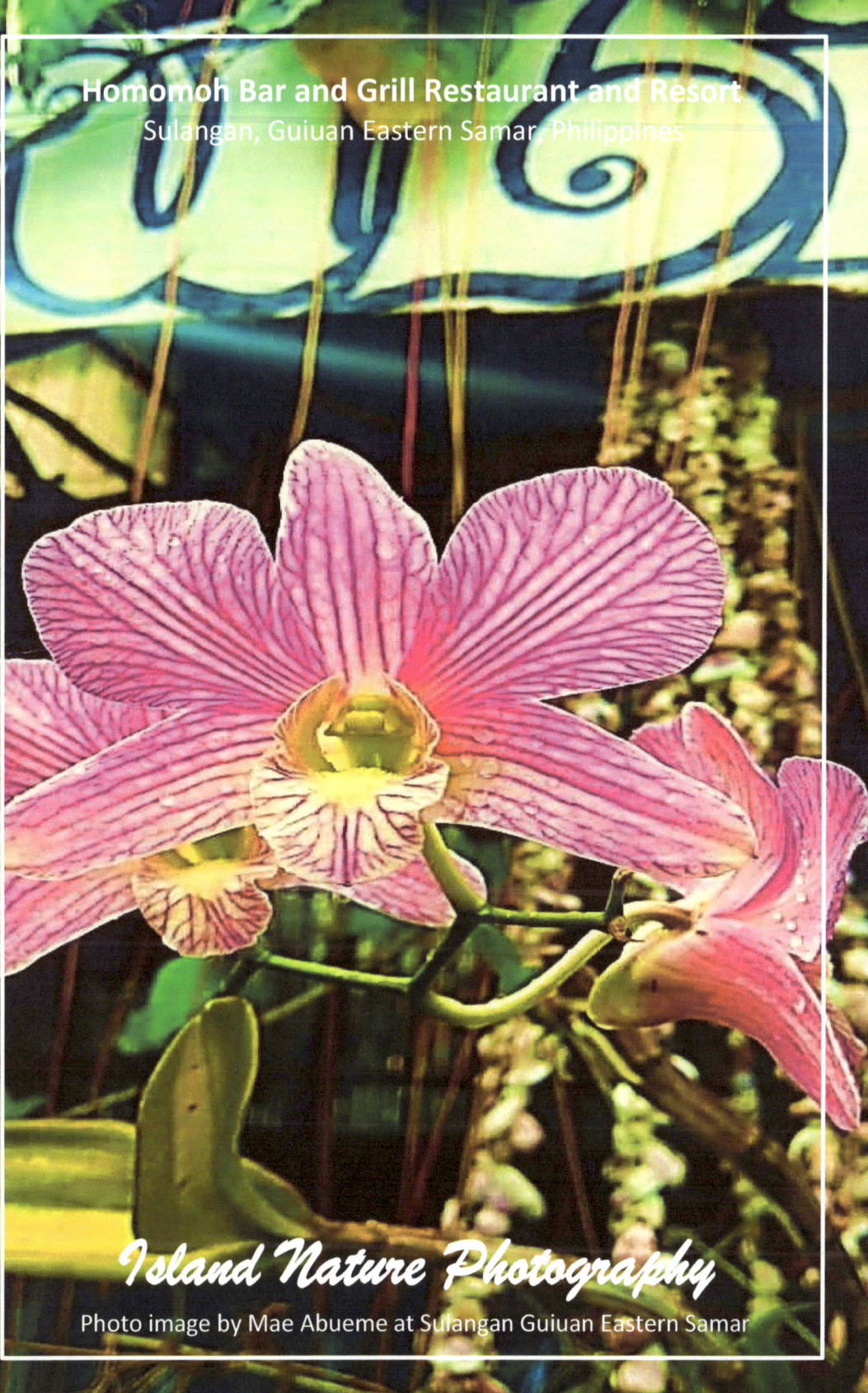

Homomoh Bar and Grill Restaurant and Resort
Sulangan, Guiuan Eastern Samar, Philippines

Island Nature Photography
Photo image by Mae Abueme at Sulangan Guiuan Eastern Samar

Homomoh Bar and Grill Restaurant and Resort
Sulangan, Guiuan Eastern Samar, Philippines

Island Nature Photography
Photo image by Mae Abueme at Sulangan Guiuan Eastern Samar

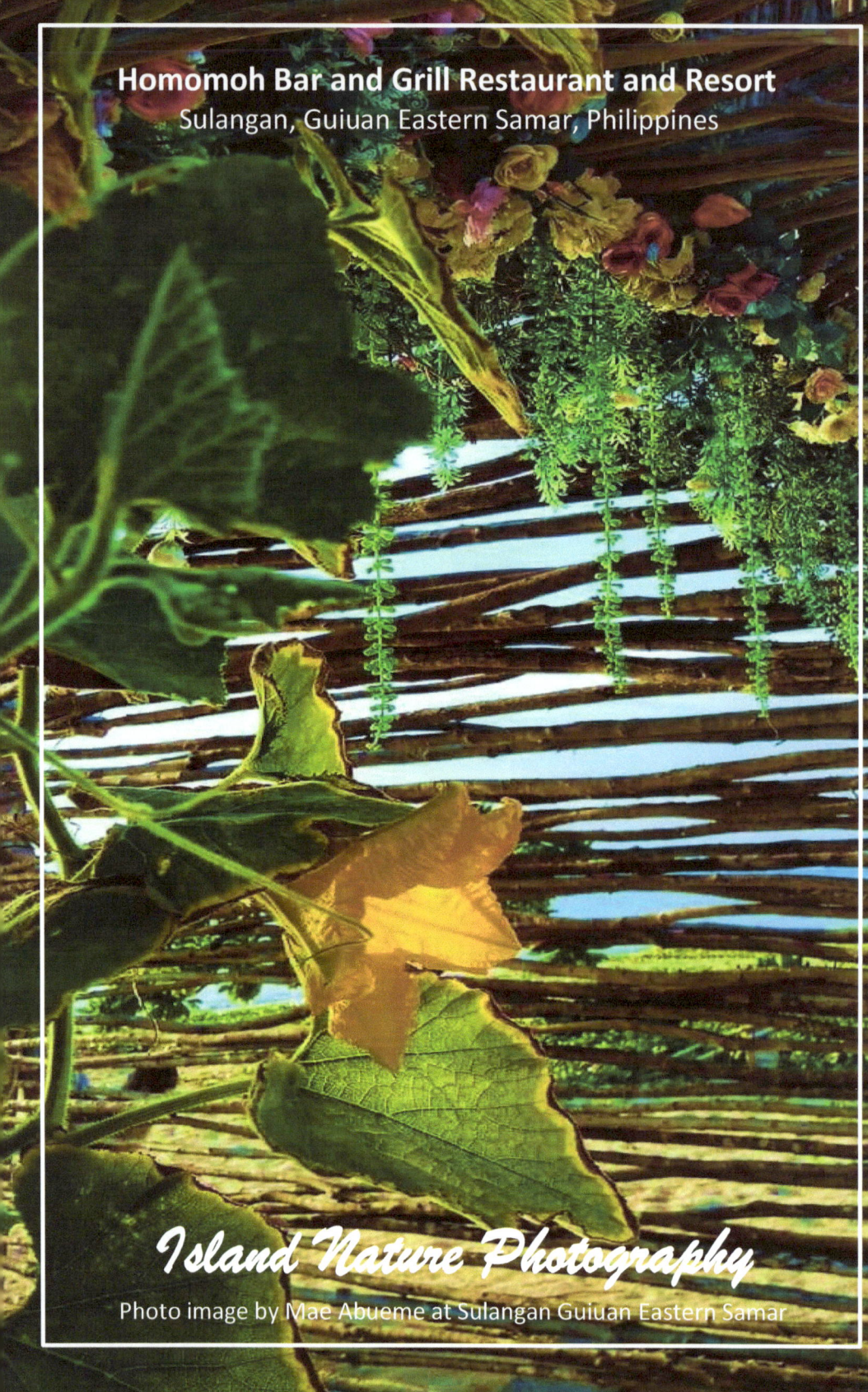

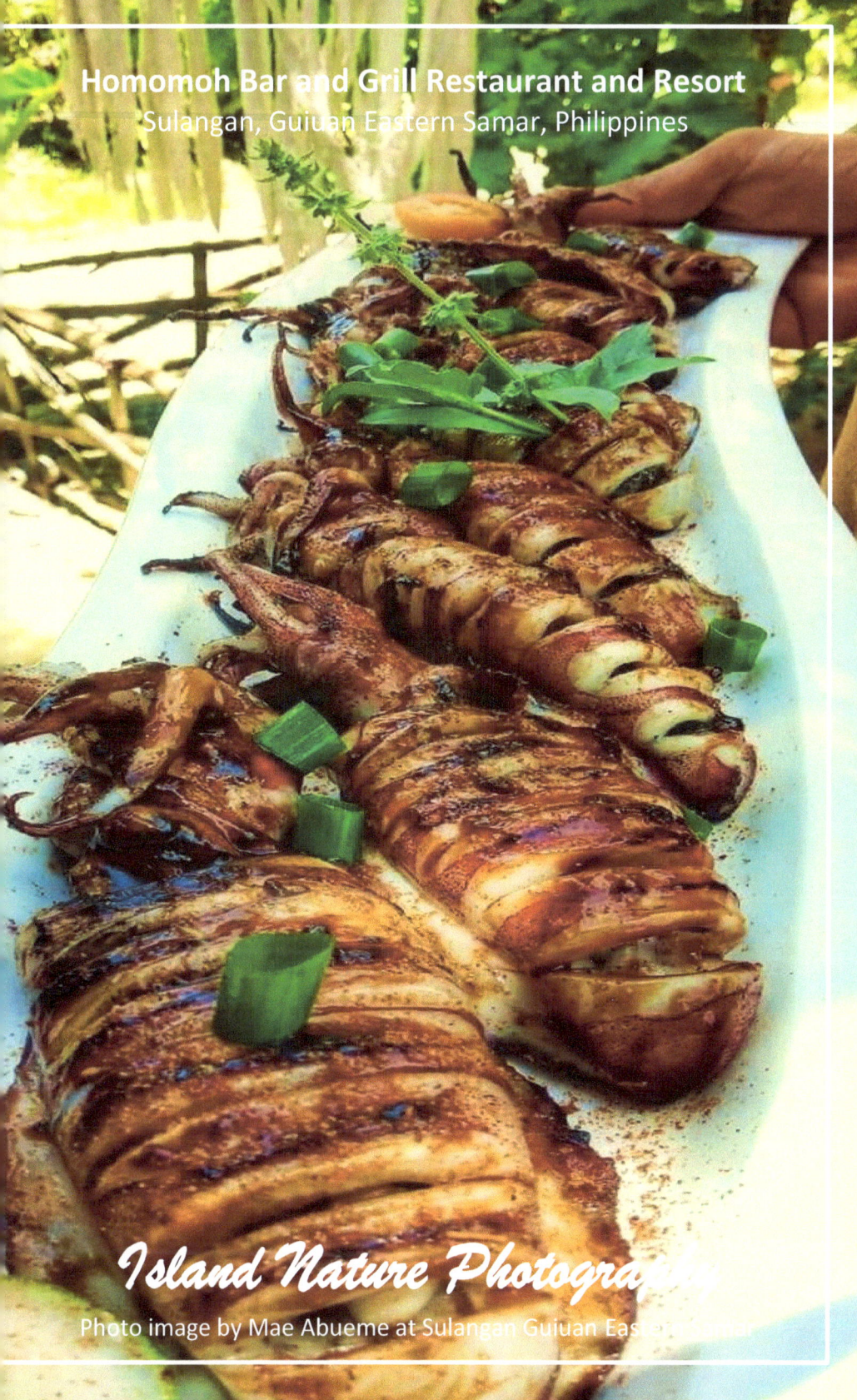

Homomoh Bar and Grill Restaurant and Resort
Sulangan, Guiuan Eastern Samar, Philippines

Island Nature Photography
Photo image by Mae Abueme at Sulangan Guiuan Eastern Samar

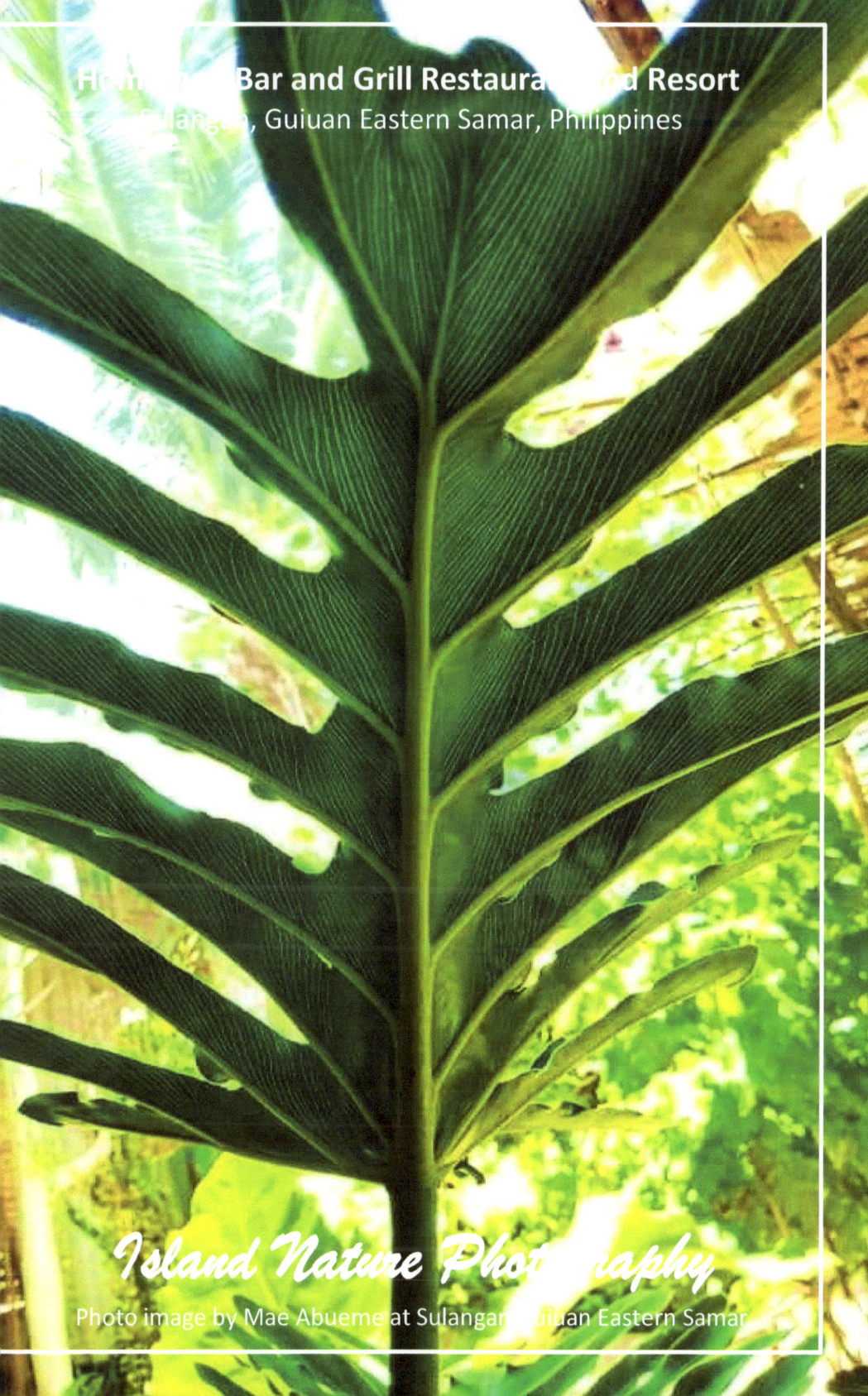

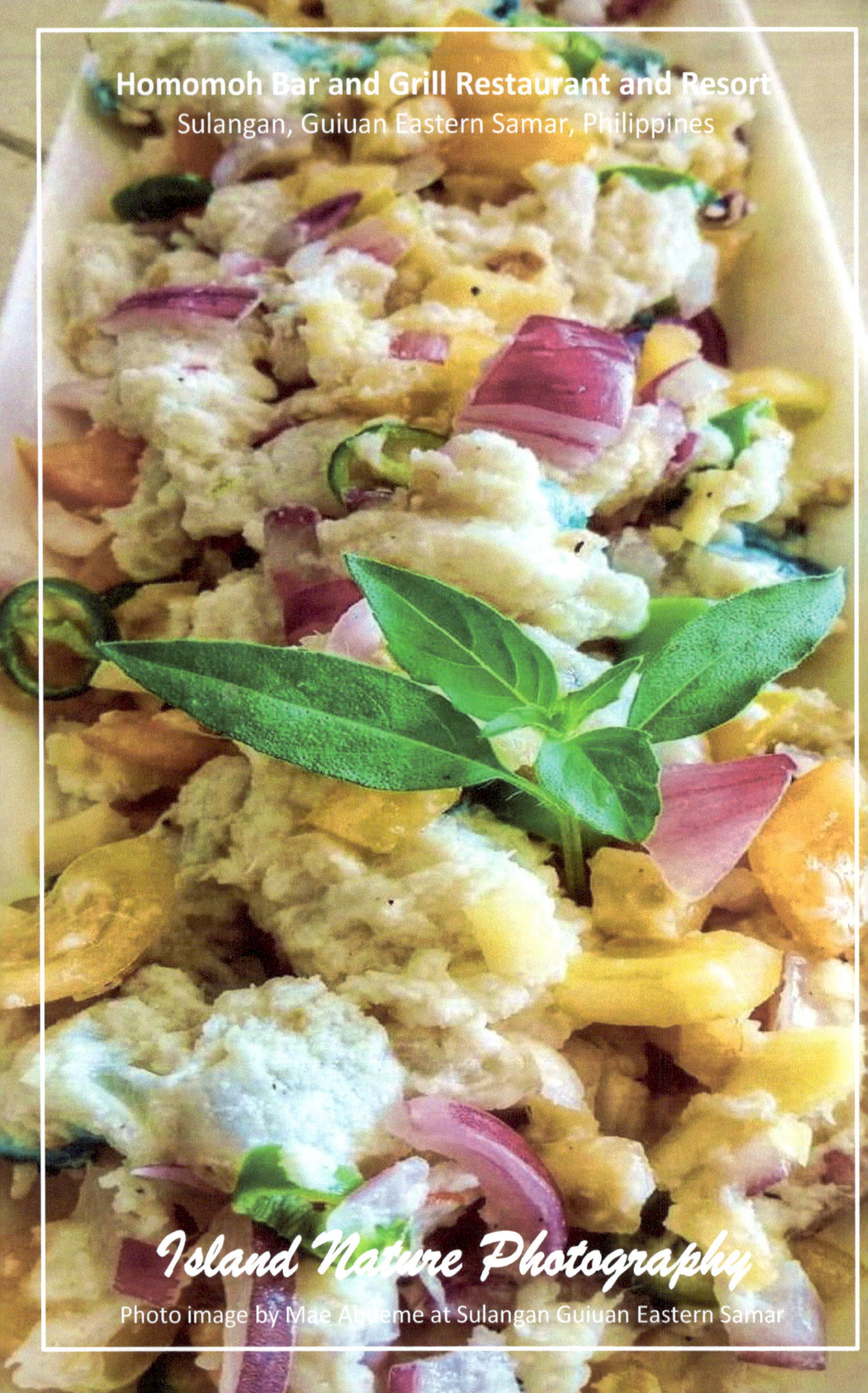

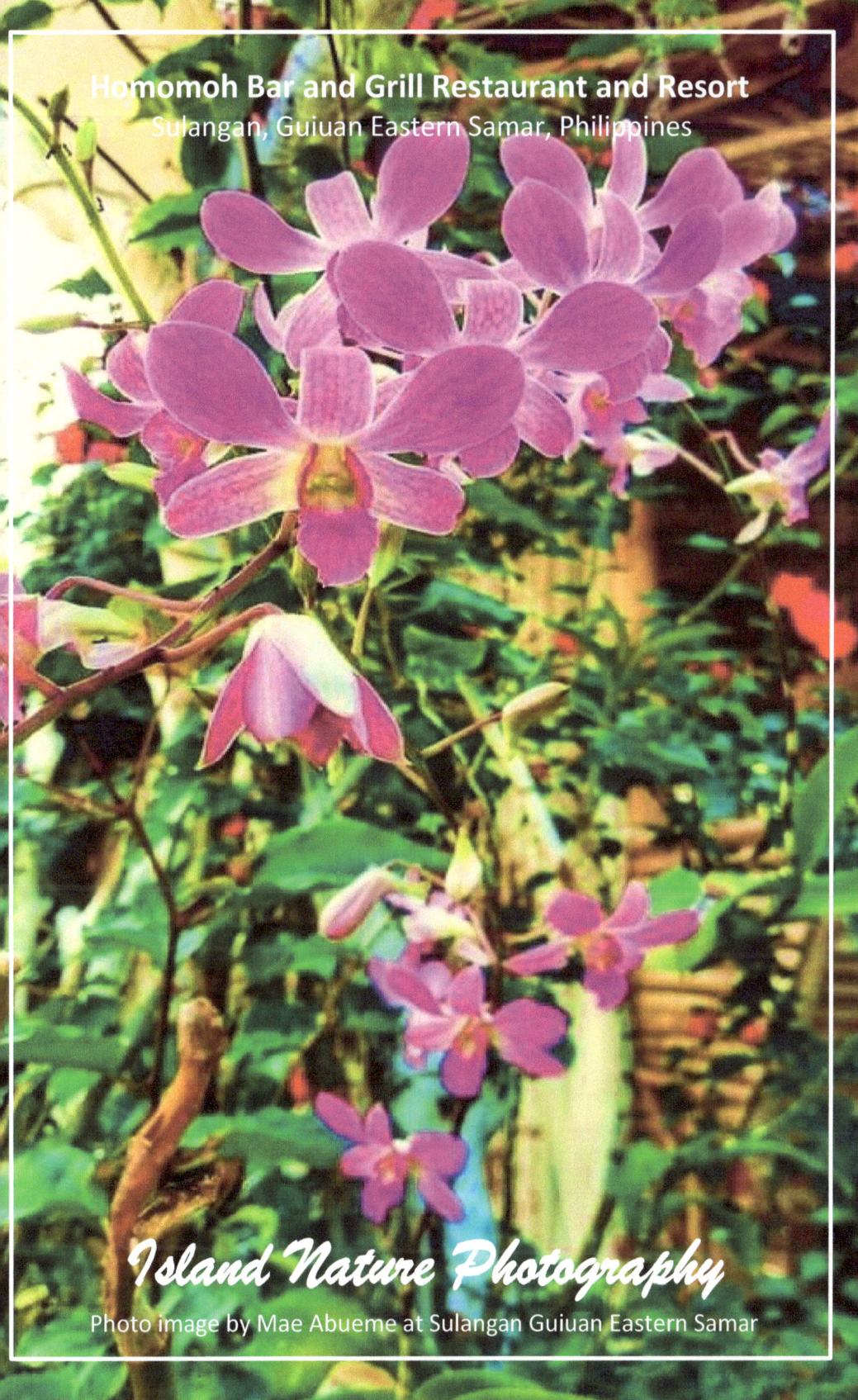

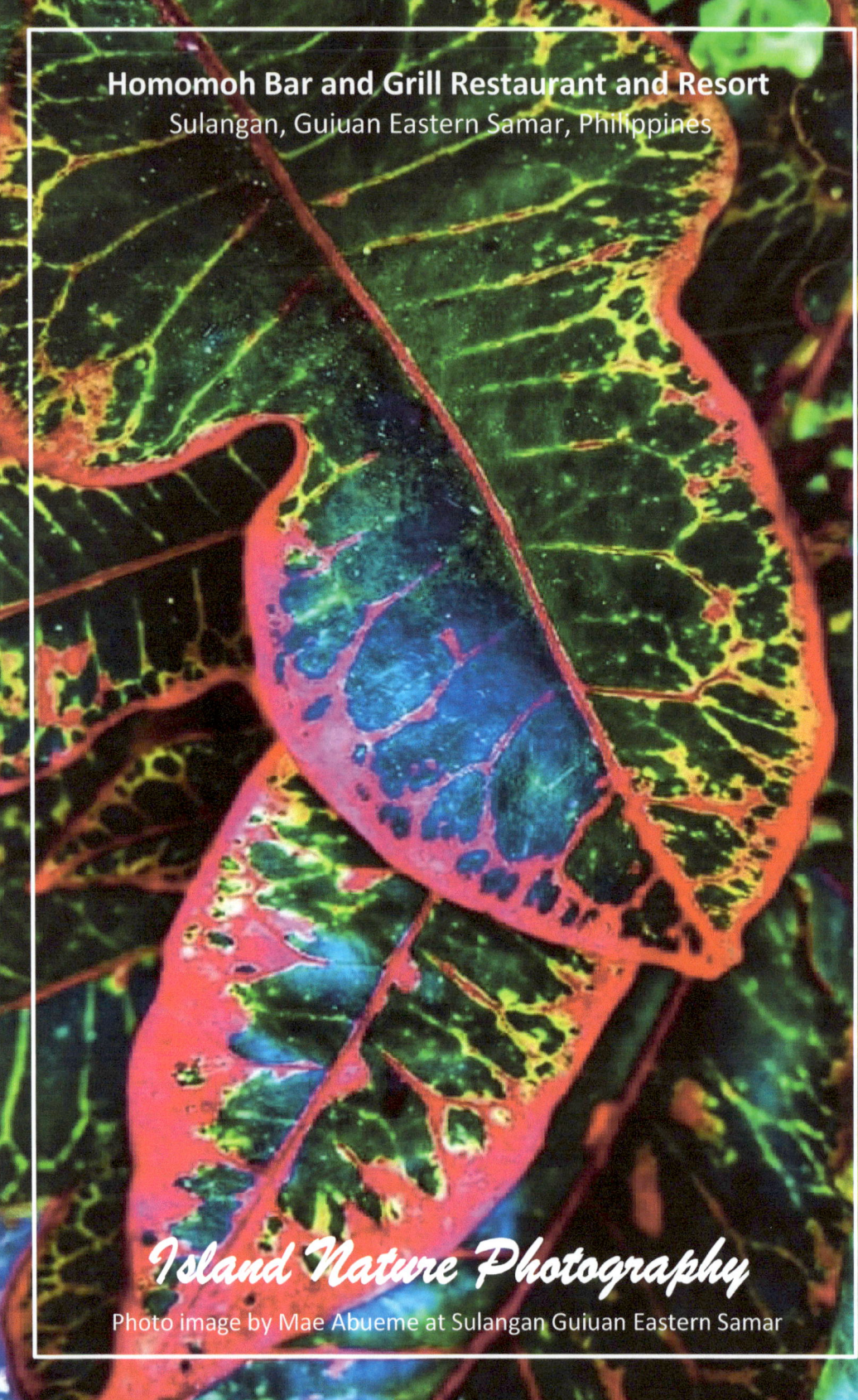

Homomoh Bar and Grill Restaurant and Resort
Sulangan, Guiuan Eastern Samar, Philippines

Island Nature Photography
Photo image by Mae Abueme at Sulangan Guiuan Eastern Samar

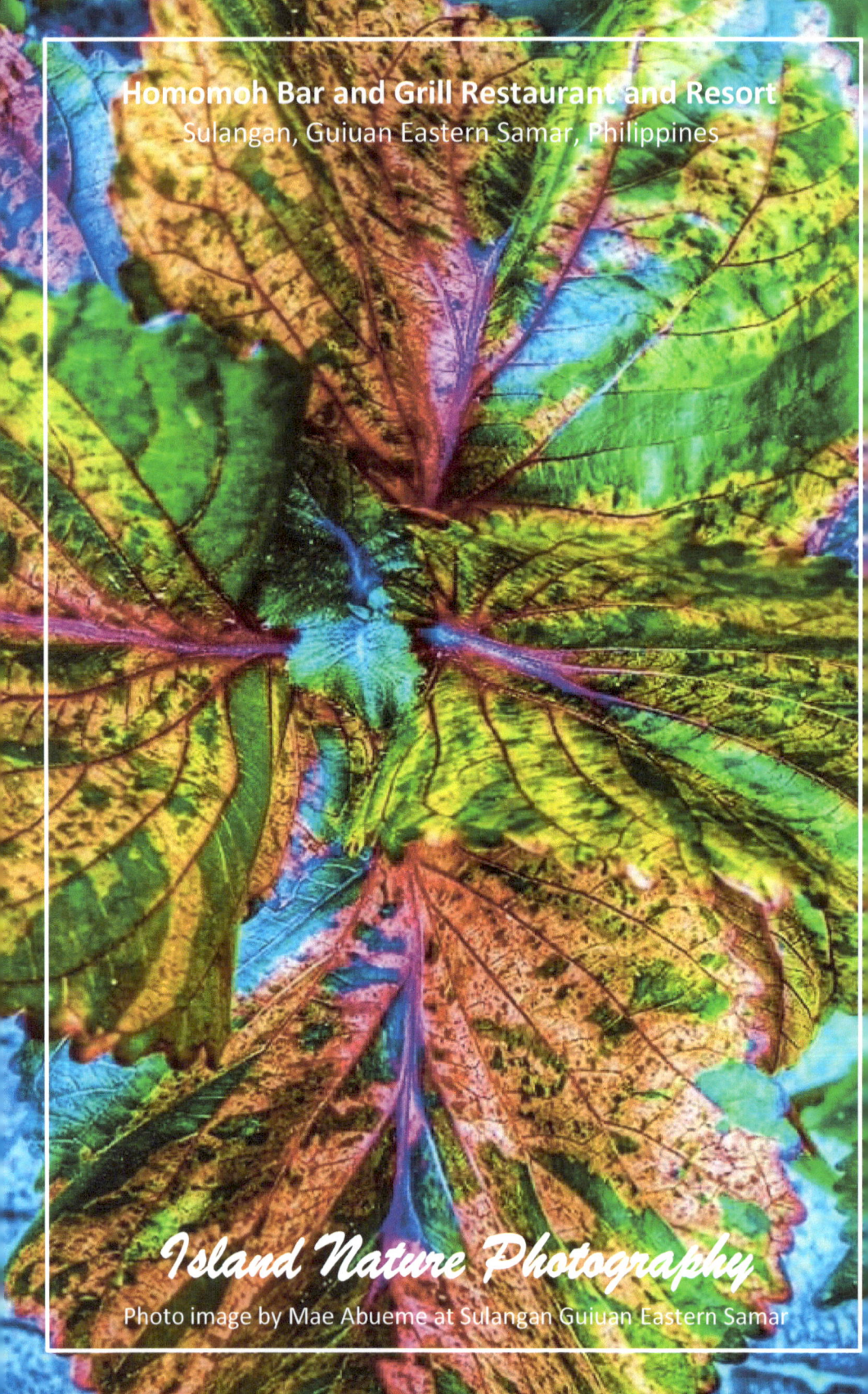

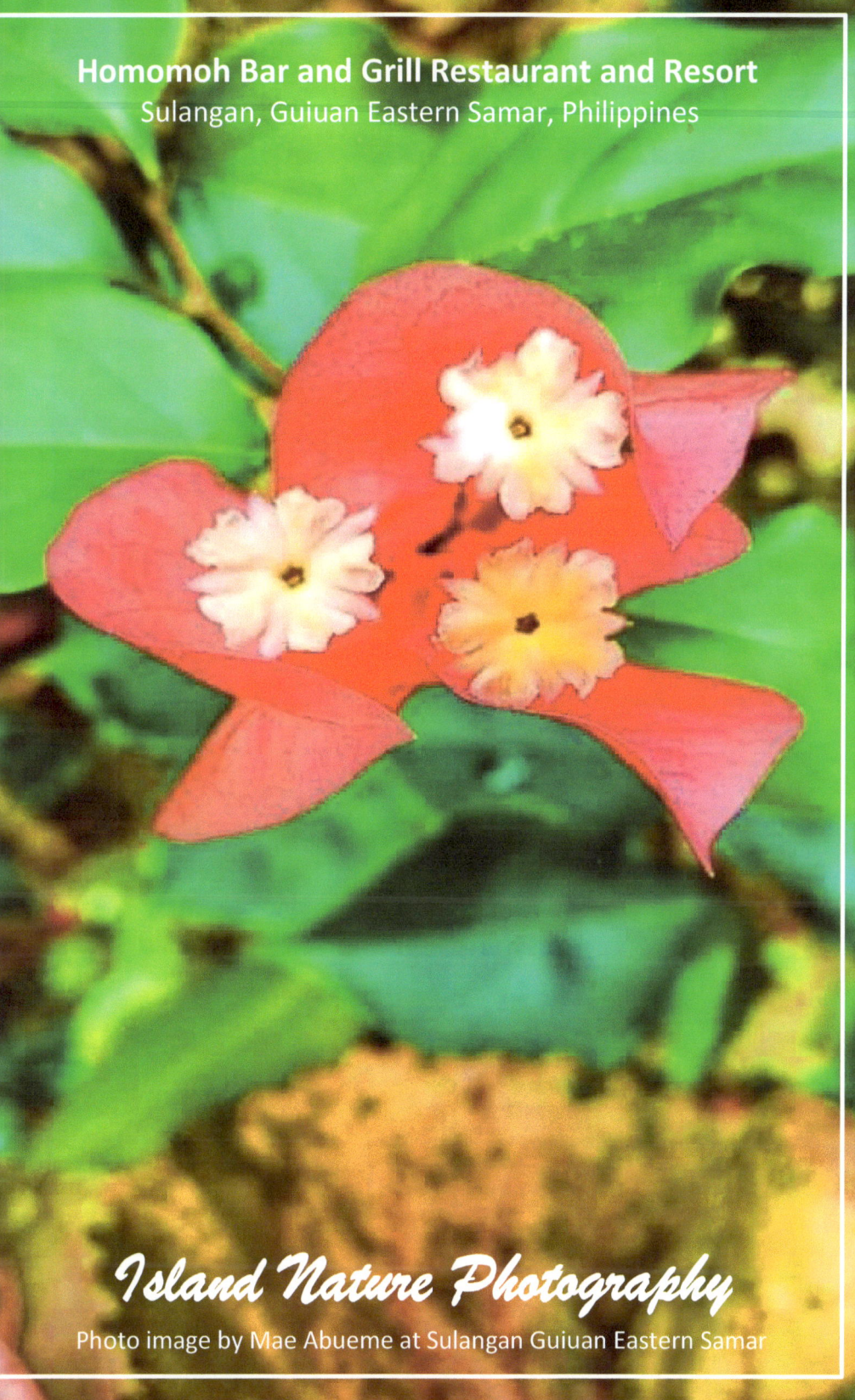

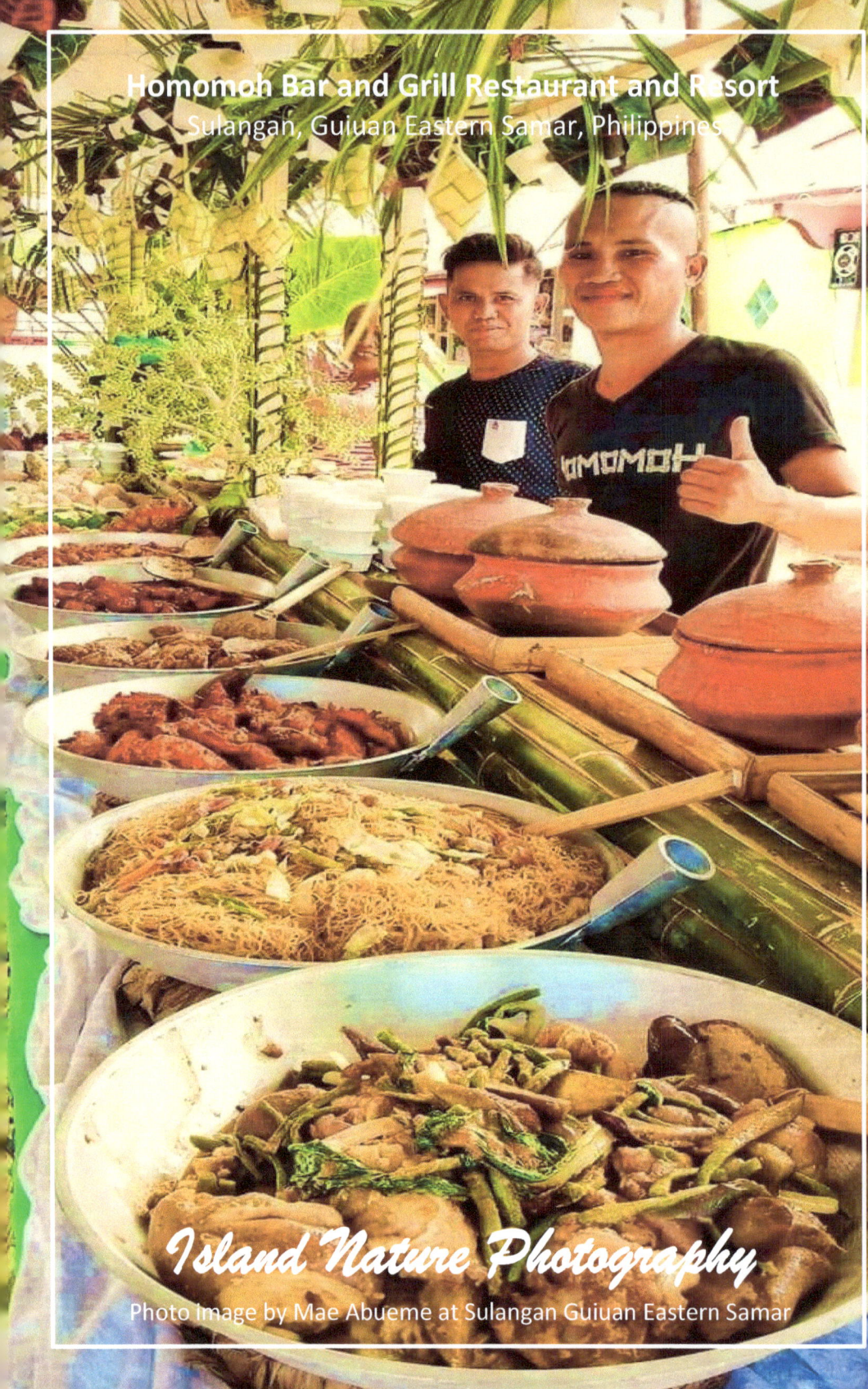

Homomoh Bar and Grill Restaurant and Resort
Sulangan, Guiuan Eastern Samar, Philippines

Island Nature Photography

Photo image by Mae Abueme at Sulangan Guiuan Eastern Samar

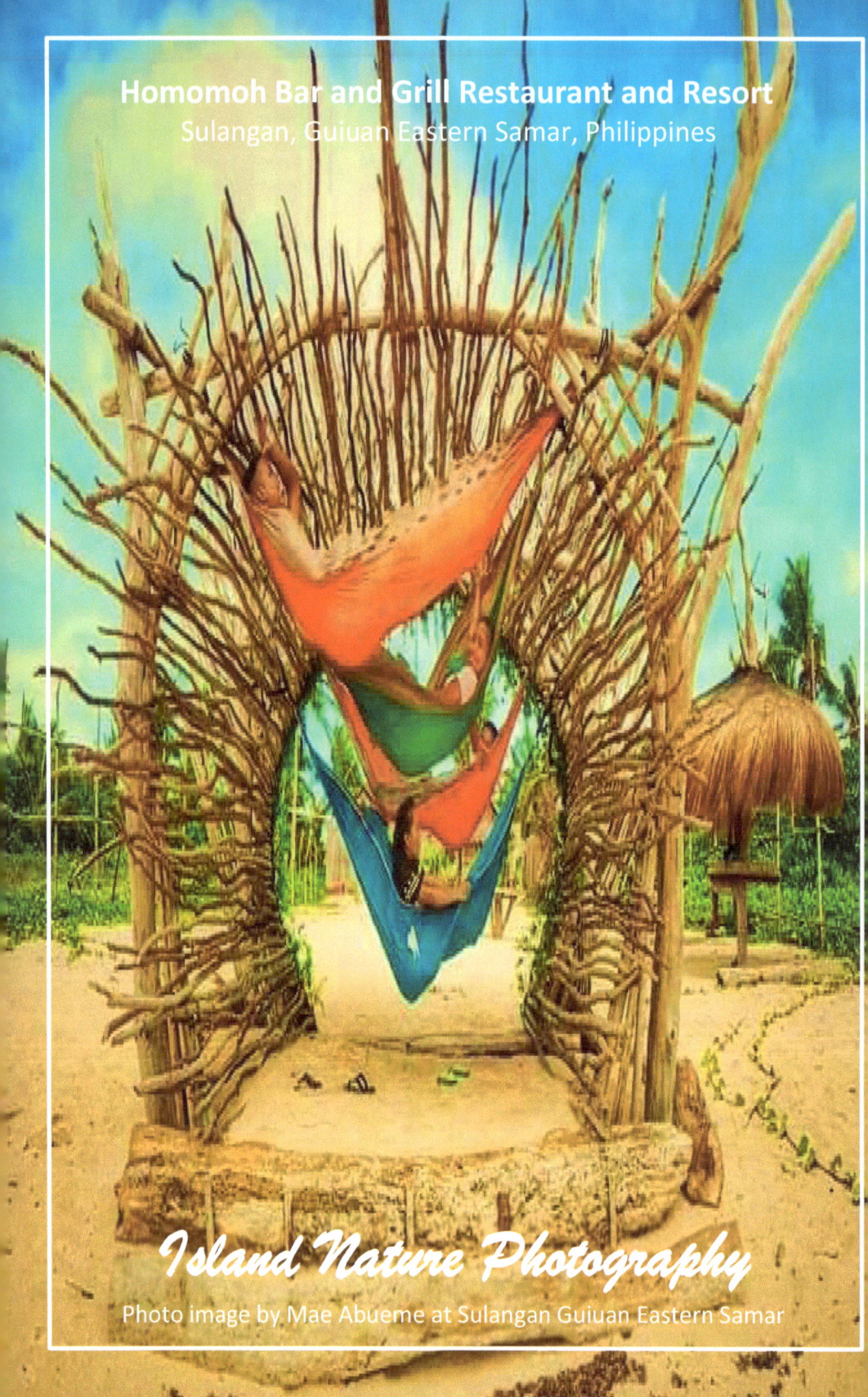

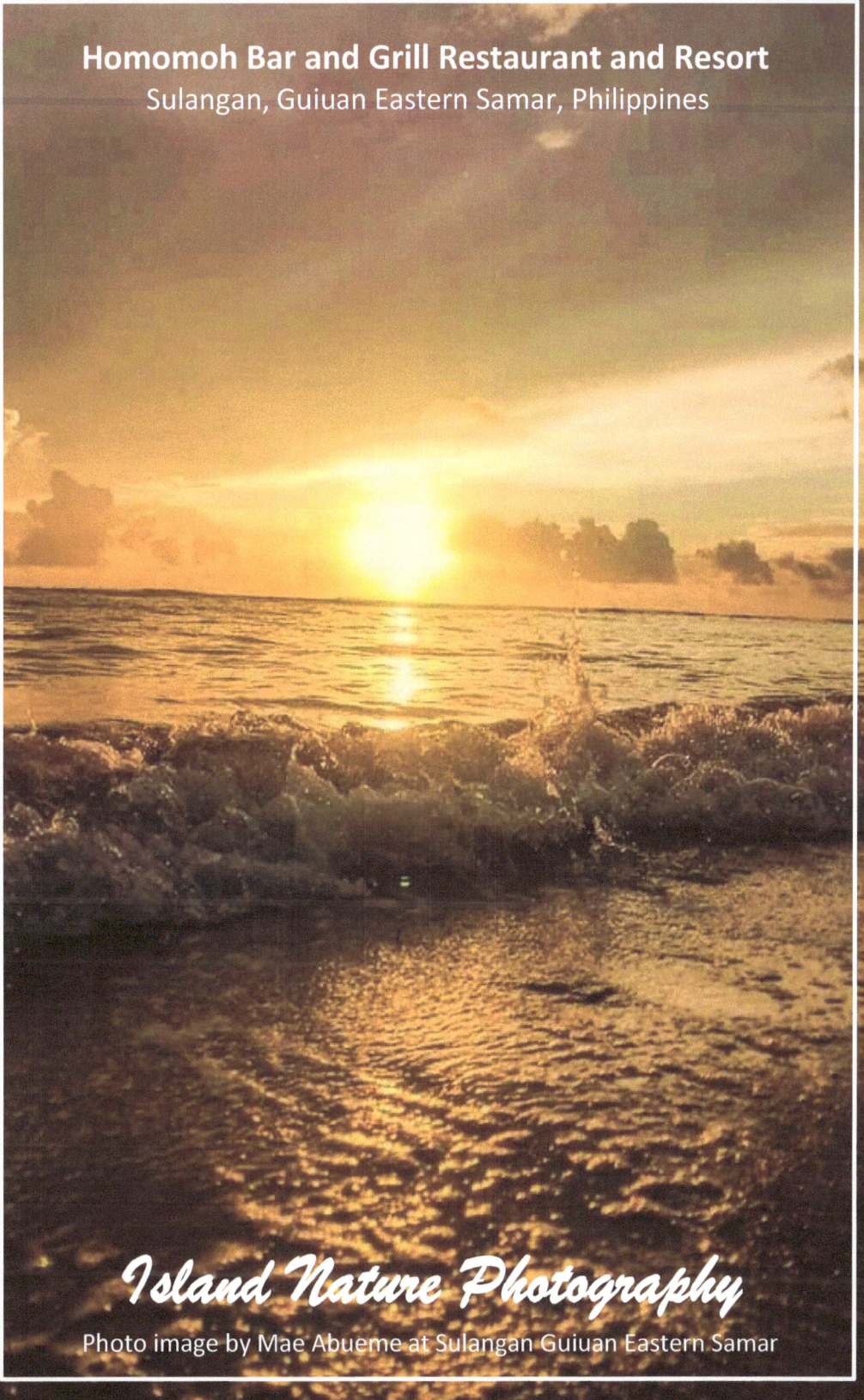

Homomoh Bar and Grill Restaurant and Resort
Sulangan, Guiuan Eastern Samar, Philippines

Island Nature Photography
Photo image by Mae Abueme at Sulangan Guiuan Eastern Samar

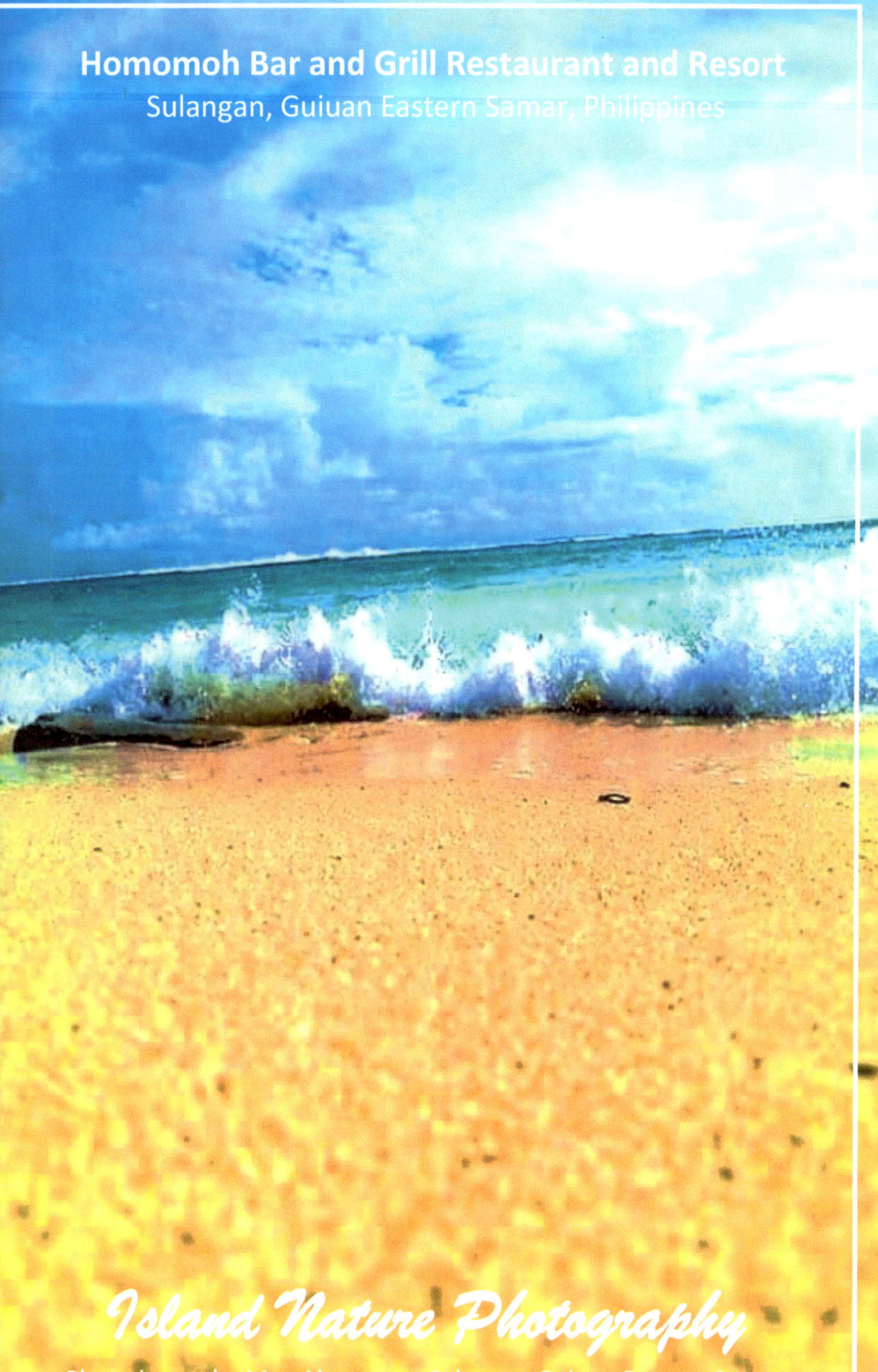

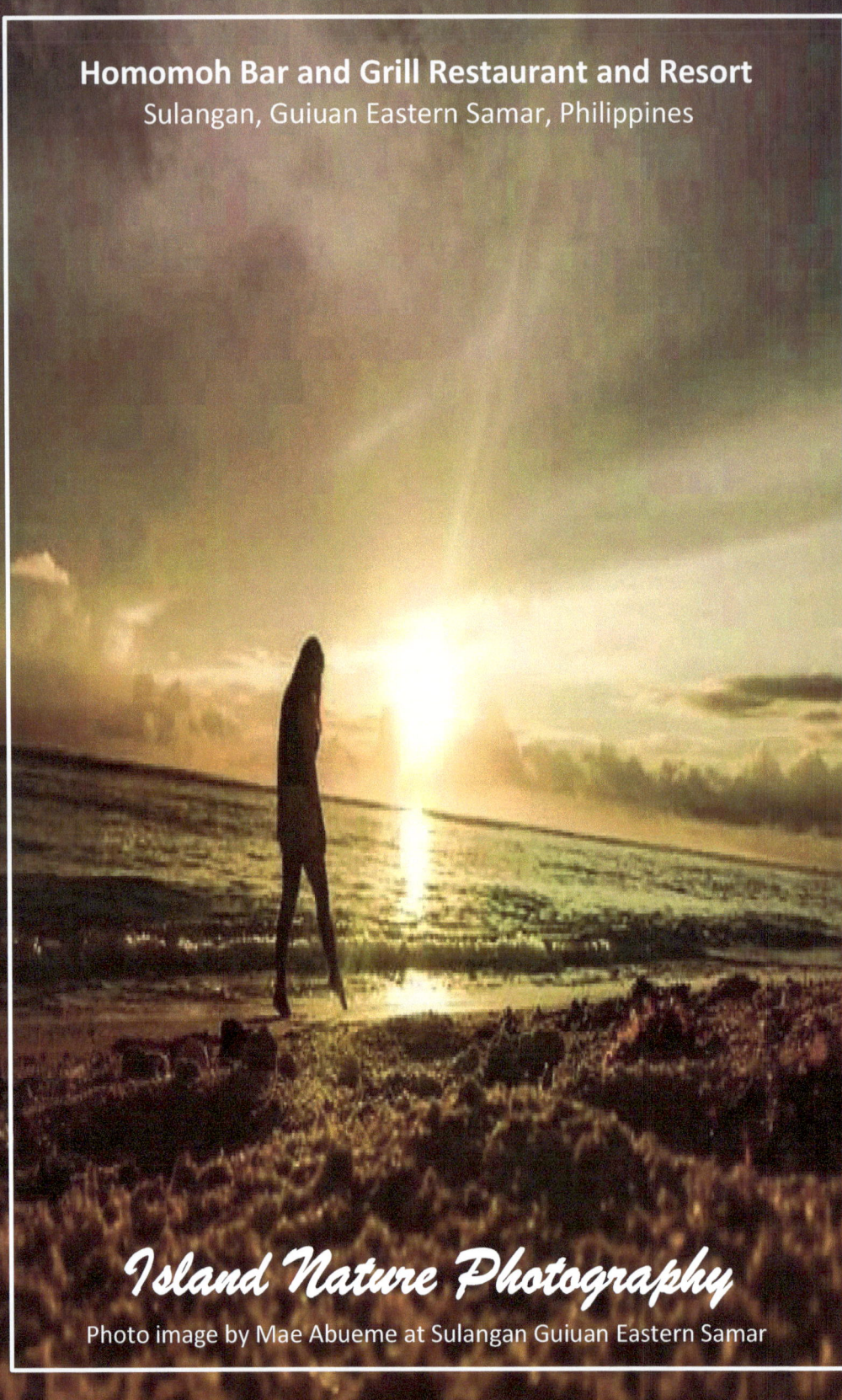

Homomoh Bar and Grill Restaurant and Resort
Sulangan, Guiuan Eastern Samar, Philippines

Island Nature Photography

Photo image by Mae Abueme at Sulangan Guiuan Eastern Samar

Homomoh Bar and Grill Restaurant and Resort
Sulangan, Guiuan Eastern Samar, Philippines

Island Nature Photography

Photo image by Mae Abueme at Sulangan Guiuan Eastern Samar

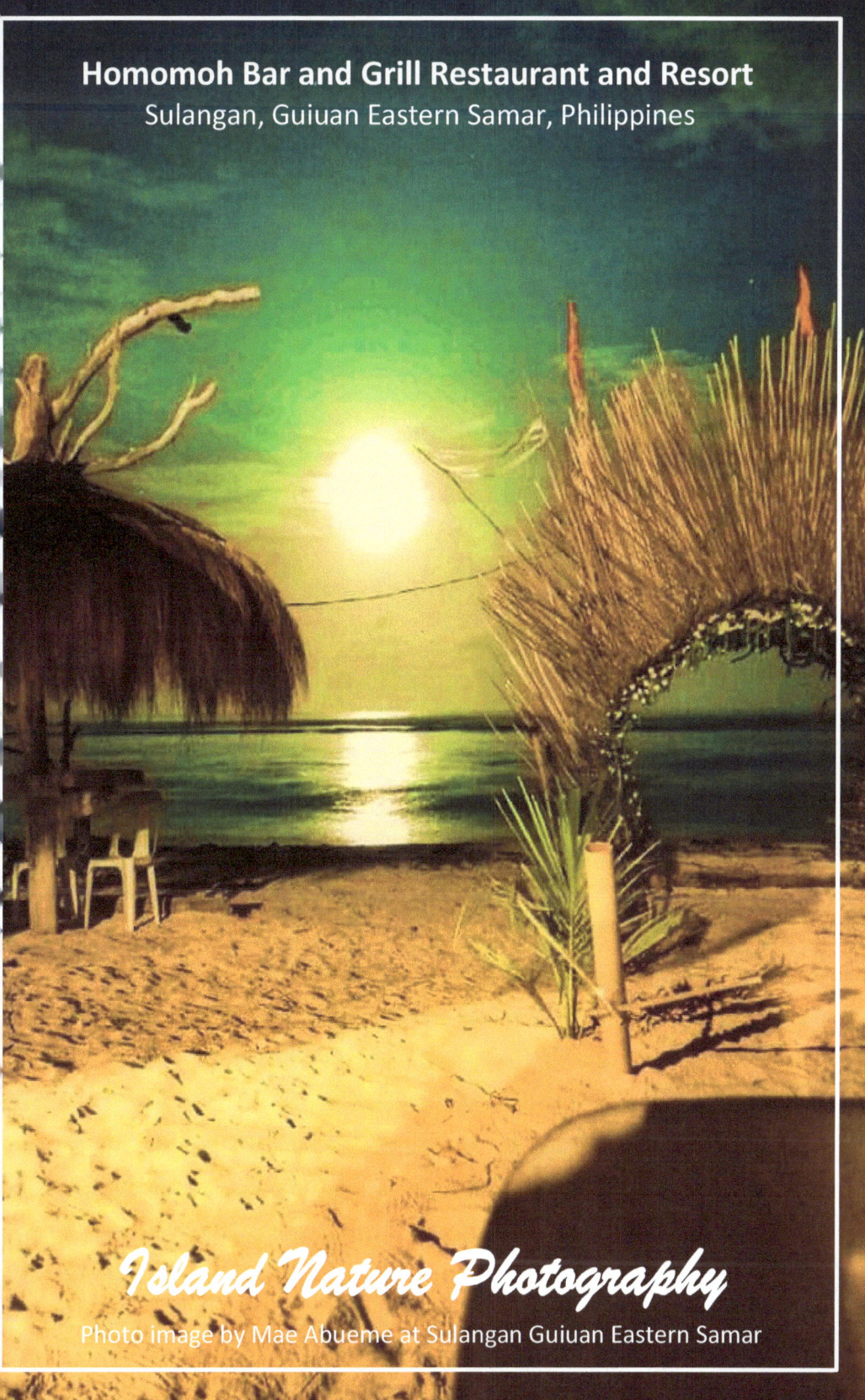

Special Thanks to

Homomoh Bar and Grill Restaurant Resort

for the Photo Images and Mae Abueme.

HOMOMOH Bar and Grill Restaurant Resort

Homomoh Bar and Grill Restaurant Resort

is Located at

Guiuan Eastern Samar, Philippines, 6809

Production Team

Photographer	**Mae Joy Abueme**
Editor	**Jeremy Ecle**

Stellar Alpha 6809 Islands Nature Photography

Stellar Alpha 6809 Productions for 2021

About the Authors

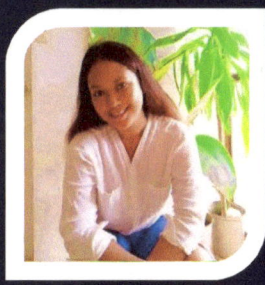

Mae Joy Abueme is a photographer, a surfer and a writer, she loves the ocean and the beauty of nature.

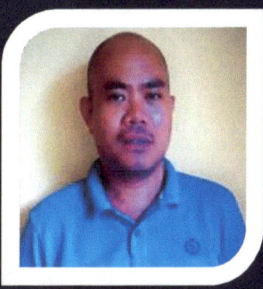

Jeremy Ecle is a photographer, a traveler a writer about nature, travels and culture.

For inquiries please email the authors at

jeremyecle2015@yahoo.com

abuememayjoy@gmail.com

Stellar Alpha 6809 Islands Nature Photography

Stellar Alpha 6809 Productions for 2021

Copyright © 2020

All rights reserved.

www.ingramcontent.com/pod-product-compliance
Lightning Source LLC
Chambersburg PA
CBHW040325220526
45473CB00009B/2570